FOR CRYING OUT LOUD!

To Kester

Happy Christmas
is hereby proclaimed
unto thee!

David Mitchell

FOR CRYING OUT LOUD!

The Story of the Town Crier and Bellman, Past and Present

David Mitchell
Town Crier and Bellman to the City of Chester

AVENUE BOOKS

First published 2010

Published by Avenue Books
P.O. Box 2118, Seaford BN25 9AR.

ISBN   978 1 905575 10 7

Internal page design by Julie Mitchell
Cover design and internal page typesetting by Richard Coan Design

Book production for the publisher by
Bookprint Creative Services, <www.bookprint.co.uk>
Printed in Great Britain.

CONTENTS

LIST OF ILLUSTRATIONS

LIST OF ILLUSTRATIONS

ACKNOWLEDGEMENTS

In the Book of Proverbs it states, 'Plans fail for lack of counsel, but with many advisers they succeed'. In the writing of this book I have taken that advice very much to heart and have drawn on the support of many advisers. In fact I have surrounded myself with arguably the most intelligent, discerning, generous-hearted and good-looking group of advisers ever assembled. They have encouraged me, detected errors, given constructive feedback and generally made the whole process less lonely than it would otherwise have been. I want to express my heartfelt thanks to these goodly folk, not only because I am genuinely grateful, but also because they will be that much more likely to rush out and buy multiple copies of the book. I do therefore publicly proclaim my indebtedness unto Geoff Brown, Irene Brown, Mark Brown, Mark Buchanan, Debbie Catt, Sue Dennis, Ruth Duffet, Tom Harrison, Clint Heacock, Rachel Macdonald, Peter Mansfield, Jayne Mowles, John Prokopiw, Brian Squires, Trevor Stephenson, Joy Tyler, Craig Wakeling and Chris Wilson.

Many people have generously assisted me in my research. I gratefully record my debt to Dr William J. Ashworth (School of History, University of Liverpool), Lonza Atkin (former Town Crier of Lichfield), Peter Axworthy, John Benson (Archivist, Cheshire Archives and Local Studies), Allen Bills (Town Crier of Bristol), Wendy M. A. Bowen (Hampshire Museums Service), Denise Brace (Huntly House Museum, Edinburgh), David Bullock (City Crier of Norwich), William Davyce, Mark Collier (Senior Lecturer in Egyptology, University of Liverpool), Ted Davy (Town Crier of Grimsby), Gordon Emery (Chester historian), Derek Fairhurst, Victoria Goodwin (Archivist, Bury St Edmunds Record Office), Tom Hand (Chester Tour Guide), Marie Henke (Photo Archivist, Nantucket Historical Association Research Library), Steve Howe (Chester historian and guide), Edward Hussey (All Souls College, Oxford), Tom Jones (Chester Tour Guide), Malcolm S. Loveday (Chairman, The Chertsey Society), Lynne Mullen (St Sepulchre's Church), Maureen Nield, Bob Partridge (Editor of Ancient *Egypt* magazine), Elaine Pierce-Jones (Chester History & Heritage), David R. Smith (Dalkeith historian), John

Smith (Town Crier of Dalkeith), Brian Sylvester (Town Crier of Newbury), Rob Tremain (Town Crier of Launceston), John Whittle (Editor, *Waverton, A History of its People and Places*) and Brenda Willison (Town Crier of Bakewell).

The search for appropriate photographs and illustrations would have been much more difficult were it not for the kind assistance I was given by David Atkinson (Cheshire West & Chester Council), Stuart Bogg (*Chester Chronicle*), Kevin Hughes, Rick Matthews (*The Chester Leader*), Laura Summerton (Bridgeman Art Library) and Robert Ward. To each of them I hereby make known my loud and grateful thanks.

Albert Rusling of The Cartoon Gallery, Chester, kindly drew the cartoon for the *Abdominal Resonators* chapter, thus giving shape and uplift to an area that would otherwise have fallen flat.

It is crucial that the cover design should capture the book's personality. Richard Coan has achieved this perfectly.

David Nickalls of Bookprint has been endlessly gracious, patient and encouraging towards this new author. I couldn't have wished for better.

I am grateful to Kenny Boyle of VisitBritain for kindly contributing the Foreword, in which he locates the town crier tradition within Britain's history and heritage. I marvel at the way he has commended this book whilst somehow avoiding the seemingly inevitable clichés: 'utterly compelling', 'literary masterpiece' and 'instant classic'.

Particular mention must be made of my niece, Helen Mitchell, who has combined encouragement and astute observation in equal measure. When I thought the book was finished, she gently and graciously prompted me to make it much better.

Brian Carter couldn't have been more committed to this project. I so much appreciate his attention to detail. I am especially grateful for his insightful suggestions and the way he has patiently introduced the wonders of computer technology to someone like me who has made a career out of preserving the oldest information technology: the handbell and scroll.

In John Spencer I have long been blessed with as good a friend as it is possible for a man to have. He has freely given his insight and encouragement to this project with the same generosity that he has contributed to virtually every enterprise that I have been involved in for the past 30 years. No words could begin to measure my gratitude to him and for him.

My father-in-law, Alan Brown, has freely passed on the expertise he has accumulated in a lifetime working as a proof-reader, printer and cartoonist. I am grateful for his input in all these areas, and especially for the delightful cartoons that he has drawn for this book.

I would need an entire chapter to record all the ways in which my wife, and fellow town crier, Julie, has contributed to this book that you have so discerningly purchased. So I will highlight just some of them. Julie has read multiple drafts of every chapter and made numerous useful suggestions. She has contributed many of the illustrations (working from historical sources), created most of the chapter icons, and organised the layout of the book. For all of these things I am grateful. But above everything, Julie, has repeatedly done something for me without which I wouldn't have been able to write a single word: yes, day after day, hour after hour, she has helped me to find my reading glasses.

Finally I come to my son Spencer, the official Apprentice Town Crier of Chester. I thank Spencer for allowing me occasional access to the computer, and for the numerous suggestions he has made for spending the vast fortune which he fondly imagines this book will generate. And most of all I thank him for being my constant delight.

Britain ™
You're invited

FOREWORD BY KENNY BOYLE

As I write (on Thursday 12th August, 2010), Prime Minister David Cameron has this morning delivered a speech at London's Serpentine Gallery. He opened by saying, "This is not a speech I had to make. It's a speech I wanted to make". His chosen subject? Tourism.

Tourism contributes £115 billion annually to the British economy. It employs over ten per cent of the national workforce, is our fifth biggest industry and our third largest export earner. In these challenging economic times then, it's small wonder that the Prime Minister went on to say "Tourism presents a huge economic opportunity. Not just bringing business to Britain but right across Britain, driving new growth in the regions and helping to deliver the rebalancing of our national economy that is so desperately needed".

But how to realise this opportunity?

The temptation for those involved in tourism marketing in Britain is to promote the country – to both domestic and international audiences – in terms of a series of contrasting (and hopefully, compelling) juxtapositions. Urban and rural. Traditional and modern. Coast and countryside. Heritage and pop. Glyndebourne and Glastonbury. It's a perfectly reasonable approach – after all few countries in the world can match the variety of Britain's tourism offering; and, in a country which is some forty times smaller than the US, this makes for a potent promotional narrative.

However, some seven years' experience with the UK's national tourism agency, VisitBritain (first as marketing director, then commercial director) tells me that, in this country of 'many parts', some parts resonate with consumers more strongly than others. For the truth is that, irrespective of its enormous continued contribution to modern global culture, this small island is the world's sixth most popular tourism destination because of its even richer history and heritage. In market research groups in country after country, consumers use different languages to convey a common view: what they want most from a visit to the UK is to experience our cultural heritage; colourful traditions; and authentic, 'living' history.

Surely there is no more perfect embodiment of these sought-after characteristics, than the town crier – a contention which is readily supported by the delighted reactions of those visitors who are fortunate to encounter one of the 200 or so criers active in Britain today.

I have been astonished to learn that the role of the town crier or bellman has never before been documented in a full-length book. How timely then that Chester's Town Crier, David Mitchell, has rectified this omission as the Prime Minister declares the future of British tourism to lie with a greater emphasis on the past. How appropriate that it is brought to us by a practising, award-winning crier, and in a style as quirky and engaging as the role he plays and the story he tells.

I am delighted to commend this book to you and to invite you to join me in celebrating the rich heritage of this popular and colourful tradition – one which has roots in classical antiquity and which is practised around the world; and yet which resolutely captures the essence of 'living' British history.

Kenny Boyle, Visit Britain
Director, Commercial and Distribution

INTRODUCTION

There's many a bygone trade that we are content to consign to history. No one today seeks to revive the role of the tallow chandler, for instance, nor that of the dog-whipper or the nightsoil man. But the image of a town crier is one that captures the imagination. This is why, despite being in this age of exploding information technology, more and more towns and cities are appointing town criers to bring the human touch to their public image and visitor welcome.

I share that fascination. I live in the historic and picturesque city of Chester, and back in the 1980s I loved to watch the town crier make his proclamations for the crowds that gathered at the High Cross. There was something about the costumed, bell-ringing, bellowing theatricality of the whole thing that captivated me. I was a primary school teacher at the time, and eventually got to know that town crier, the good-hearted, larger-than-life Mike Chittenden. I even invited him into the schools where I taught, to demonstrate his vocal prowess to the children, never dreaming that I would one day step into his shoes.

But through a bizarre chain of circumstances – a disguise that Providence often wears – I eventually became Chester's town crier. Even more strangely, my wife, and then my son, also donned tricorne hats and buckled shoes. We became a whole family of town criers.

I was obviously aware that town criers played a significant role in daily life before newspapers, as did the bellmen. Being an avid reader, it naturally occurred to me to go into my local library to read up on the heritage of which I had now become a part. To my surprise, there were no books on the subject. I even requested books from the British Lending Library, but again was told there was nothing.

This was indeed strange. For most of English history, news of all kinds has been spread by word of mouth. Shakespeare lived and died without ever having read a newspaper. Instead, the significant events of his time were 'published and proclaimed'[1] by the town crier or bellman. Even the death of Elizabeth I, and the contentious succession of James I, was announced by the unamplified human voice.

Today the office of town crier is not only one of Britain's oldest civic offices, it is also one that, perhaps more than any other, appeals to the public, and especially to tourists. Many towns and cities have retained or revived the position, despite its original purpose having been superseded by more efficient means of mass communication. It is therefore rather astonishing that no full-length book has yet been published that tells the story of these walking-talking newspapers and pioneer outside broadcasters. I decided to write the book I wanted to read.

The first part of the book traces the roles of the crier and the bellman as the forerunners of the newspaper, obituary column, lost-and-found notice, burglar alarm, smoke detector, night watchman, weather reporter, trading standards officer, speaking clock, public address system, advertising hoarding, newsreader and outside broadcaster.

The story is then brought up to date by recounting some of the adventures of a modern-day town crier. These include making public marriage proposals, perilous horseback proclamations, appearances in feature films, fielding bizarre questions from tourists, and competing in town crier championships. So come with me to explore the untold story of tricorne hats, buckled shoes and men-in-tights.

David Mitchell
Town Crier of Chester

1. The Chester Town Crier and his apprentice, David and Spencer Mitchell

A Note to the Reader

When quoting from historical sources I have largely retained the original spelling to preserve the charm and patina of antiquity. However I have modernised the spelling in some minor instances when this seemed necessary to clarify the meaning. Anyone who wishes to track down the originals may do so via the Notes and References.

Both of our key terms, 'crier' and 'bellman', were often spelt differently in earlier times, as 'cryer' and 'belman' or even 'bel-man', so I have retained these spellings when quoting from historical sources.

I have rendered these terms – crier and bellman – without capitalisation except when those words are a specific title, in which case they are capitalised, such as 'Town Crier of Chester'. The occasional exception occurs when these words occur within an historical quotation, in which case I have preserved the usage of the original author.

Any other misspellings within the text, or indeed any errors of any kind, are oversights. Be assured that my proof-reader will spend a day and a night in the stocks at the High Cross, Chester, for each and every error found within. There – as a seventeenth-century town crier put it – 'let him take what comes!' [2]

PART 1
THE GENERAL HISTORY

1

DISTANT ECHOES

Even in my lifetime England has suffered ignominious defeats. I shudder, for example, to recall the moment we lost on penalties to Germany in the semi-finals of the 1990 World Cup, when Chris Waddle ballooned the ball over the bar. In earlier times his life would not have been so readily spared. But perhaps England's most disastrous defeat – and certainly the one with the most far-reaching consequences for the history of town crying – was the home defeat against the little-fancied Norman-French side at Hastings in 1066. Of course we wouldn't have lost at all if the Normans hadn't cheated. We were enjoying by far the better of the early exchanges until the devious French striker, William, stuck his elbow into our skipper's eye (some translations render 'elbow' figuratively as 'arrow').

Defeat was bad enough, but far worse was that the French didn't go back home after the match. Camembert and garlic quickly spread across our hitherto green and pleasant land. And thus it was that from 1066 the words 'Oyez . . . OYEZ! . . . **OYEZ!**' began to be heard within these shores. It is a strange but common phenomenon. We meet someone who doesn't speak our language so we think we can *make* him understand by repeating the same unfamiliar words louder and louder: 'Oyez . . . OYEZ! . . . **OYEZ!**'

So we can certainly trace back to our French conquerors the three Oyez's (the Norman-French equivalent of 'Hearken') which traditionally preface every proclamation. But that's as far as I'm prepared to go. There is a parallel claim often made for William the Conqueror that I want to contest. Several popular history books state that William introduced town criers into England in the wake of his conquest. The story goes that he appointed criers to travel throughout the land, announcing his victory and proclaiming his laws.

Let me ask you, *mon ami*, does this stand to reason? Is it at all plausible? We had already been resourcefully innovative before 1066. We had long since built Stonehenge, carved white horses into chalk hillsides, created exquisite illuminated manuscripts, and learnt to make manuscript ink by mixing powdered oak galls with monks' urine. With this level of native ingenuity, would we really have needed a bunch of foreigners with odd pronunciation to come over here to say, 'Av yoo nevere sort ov avving sumone stand in ze market skware and shout ze news to ze people wen zay ar all gazzairred togezzaire in won pless?' After all, other civilisations had fastened onto this blindingly-obvious procedure centuries previously, as we will shortly discover.

2. Bayeux Tapestry out-take

Before finally dismissing the claim that William the Conqueror introduced criers to Britain, we must first address the conclusion sometimes wrongly drawn from the Bayeux Tapestry. It is true that two bellmen are indeed to be seen on the tapestry which so vividly depicts the Conquest. However, the evidence proves precisely the opposite of what is often claimed. The scene in which bellmen appear is one which depicts Britain *prior* to the Norman invasion. The body of Edward the Confessor, on a richly-decorated bier, is being carried to his final resting place, the Church of St Peter, in January 1066, ten months before the Battle of Hastings. The two bellmen are accompanying the funeral procession. The legitimate conclusion to be drawn, therefore, is that the tradition of bellmen accompanying funeral processions was already well-established in Britain *before* the Conquest.

3. Two bellmen accompany the funeral procession of Edward the Confessor

Many people assume that having town criers is a peculiarly British tradition. Not so. Public announcements, made in public places by a loud and clear human voice, were essential in all cultures prior to the advent of modern mass media. It was equally inevitable that people particularly well-equipped to cry aloud should be chosen for the task, and therefore undertake proclaiming as their profession.

4. Demosthenes, 'the perfect orator', with scroll in hand

The Athens of Ancient Greece is well known as the birthplace of democracy. Less well known is that if Athens was the birthplace, then the Greek town crier was the midwife who brought democracy into the world. To participate in the democratic process, the free citizens of the Greek city-state had to gather together for the assembly, or *ekklesia*, and there participate in self-government. It was the Greek crier who went round calling the free citizens out of their houses to attend the *ekklesia* (ek is out, plus *kalein*, to call or cry). Thus we find the crier playing an essential role right at the birth of democracy.

Aristotle also emphasised the central value of the crier when he advocated that the ideal size of a Greek city-state should not be larger than that over which a shouting human voice can make itself heard. In other words Aristotle himself advocated that Greek city-states should be deliberately planned within the vocal range of a crier. How discerning of him.

Less idealistically, the crier in Ancient Greece had a central role to play in matters of foreign policy. He would be called upon to declare war or proclaim peace. One assumes this kind of proclamation was not without its dangers. Presumably such criers often resorted to the Ancient Greek equivalent of 'Don't shoot the messenger!'

One mythological crier has become synonymous with crying out loud – Stentor. In the war against Troy, as told in Homer's *Iliad*, Stentor was reputed to be as loud as fifty ordinary men combined. Useful on the battlefield no doubt, but not the sort of person you'd want moving in next door. And Demosthenes, whom Cicero called 'the perfect orator', famously trained his voice for public speaking by declaiming verse whilst running uphill, speaking

24

with pebbles in his mouth, and trying to make himself heard above the sound of the waves on the beach.

In Ancient Rome it was the *praeco* (public crier) who carried out all the functions we commonly associate with a town crier, and one or two more besides. The *praeco* would, in various contexts, proclaim: possessions that had been lost, the time and place of forthcoming public auctions, the outcome of voting at elections, verdicts at trials, and the summoning of mourners to a funeral. All these have

5. Roman proclaimer as depicted on a coin circa 17 BC

echoes in the duties of British town criers of more recent history.

The *praeco* had at least one other characteristic in common with his British successors: a trademark preface to each cry. Whereas English-speaking criers always begin with three cries of 'Oyez!', the *praeco's* equivalent was *'Hoc agete!'* – 'Give your attention to this!'

Additionally the *praeco* in the Roman Empire would cry in some situations that have no obvious parallels in our own tradition. Such functions included summoning people to attend ceremonies at which sacrifices were to be made to Roman gods and, at the conclusion of some trials, commanding the executioner to carry out sentence – the unkindest cry of all.

We know far less about proclaimers in Ancient Egypt than those of the Graeco-Roman period, but what little we do know suggests that they had distinctive characteristics. There are several surviving examples of proclaimers reading aloud from documents within the community of Deir el-Medina, the village which housed the workers who built the tombs of the pharaohs in the Valley of the Kings. Perhaps the most intriguing example dates from the end of the Twentieth Dynasty (the end of the New Kingdom), about 1100–1050 BC. It is a letter from Piankh, the Army General and High Priest of Amun, essentially the most powerful man in Thebes at this time, to the workmen at Deir el-Medina. A scribe named Butehamun receives the letter and takes it to his village at Deir el-Medina, gathers the workers together, and reads the General's letter out loud to them. I quote from the letter:

> We have taken note of every matter which our Lord [Piankh] has written to us about. Concerning your sending of that particular letter through Hori the Sherden the retainer of our Lord [the messenger who carried the letter], the Scribe Butehamun ferried across and received it from him in Month 1 of Shemu Day 18. I assembled the two Chief Workmen, the Scribe Butehamun, the Guardian Kar, and all the Workmen of the Necropolis, and I read it out loud to them. And they said, 'We will do, we will do, as our Lord has said,' from their oldest to their youngest. [3]

So we have here a very early example of a proclaimer who is acutely conscious of the precarious nature of being the mouthpiece of a great man. We can also note that Butehamun is a man of many talents: he doubles up not only as scribe and proclaimer, but also as proclaimer and audience: 'I assembled . . . the Scribe Butehamun . . . and I [the Scribe Butehamun] read it out loud'.

This latter observation ties in with our illustration (opposite) which depicts a scribe in the act of proclaiming from the scroll that he has written. Although we don't know the proclaimer's name in this instance, we know he is also a scribe because he has under his arm a scribe's palette, holding his reed pens and red and black inks. This scene comes from the tomb of a man called Merreruka at Saqqara in Egypt and it dates to around 2330 BC. Merreruka was the Vizier to King Teti whose pyramid is close to Merreruka's own tomb. [4]

The book of ancient history with which many of us are most familiar is, of course, the Bible. I often ask Bible-readers if they have spotted town criers in the Bible. They are usually bemused. The expression 'town crier' is not to be found anywhere within its pages, nor will one find any reference to tricorne hats, buckled shoes or handbells. But if we look beyond the British traditions of vocabulary and dress, and focus instead on the core characteristics of a town crier – proclaiming loudly to people gathered

6. Egyptian scribe-proclaimer depicted on
Merreruka's tomb, circa 2230 BC

together in public places – we find criers spread throughout the Old and New
Testaments. Take for example:

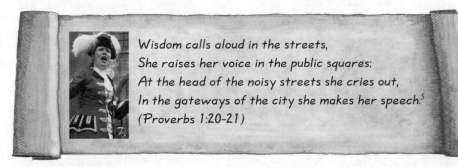

Wisdom calls aloud in the streets,
She raises her voice in the public squares;
At the head of the noisy streets she cries out,
In the gateways of the city she makes her speech.[5]
(Proverbs 1:20-21)

In this passage from *Proverbs*, completed in about 700 BC,
announcements are being made by the unamplified voice in the city's popular
gathering places. We also note the reference to a female crier (Wisdom is
personified very specifically as 'she') – a point to which my town-crier-wife,
Julie, insists I give due emphasis.

This clearly depicts a town crier in action. Admittedly there is no
reference in this passage to other key features commonly associated with town

27

criers: the use of an attention-gaining device and a scroll. But with patience we will find them in other passages.

The attention-gaining device most often used to preface a public proclamation in England is, of course, the handbell, but historically the handbell was just one of many possibilities. Several towns, notably Ripon, retain the role of hornblower, who prefaces his announcements with a blast on the ox-horn. Dutch criers traditionally used a gong; Scottish and French criers preferred the drum. In the book of Daniel, King Nebuchadnezzar's decree is so momentous that *every* available instrument is employed to give it additional authority:

Then the Herald loudly proclaimed, 'This is what you are commanded to do, O peoples, nations and men of every language: As soon as you hear the sound of the horn, flute, zither, lyre, harp, pipes and all kinds of music, you must fall down and worship the image of gold that King Nebuchadnezzar has set up.'[6]
(Daniel 3:4-5)

8.

Likewise there are many biblical references to the use of a scroll in public proclamations. Memorably the prophet Ezekiel does not merely read from a scroll, he eats it:

Son of man, eat what is before you, eat this scroll, then go and speak to the house of Israel.[7]
(Ezekiel 3:1)

So in the Old Testament we find not only public proclamations from a scroll, but also this literal application of the instruction 'read, mark, learn and inwardly digest'.

Very early in the New Testament Jesus begins his public ministry by declaring himself to be a proclaimer. In Luke we read that when Jesus went back to Nazareth, his childhood home, he went to the synagogue,

> where the scroll of the prophet Isaiah was handed to him. Unrolling it, he found the place where it is written: `...
> He has sent me to proclaim freedom for the prisoners, the recovery of sight to the blind... to proclaim the year of the Lord's favour'.[8]
> (Luke 4:16-19)

We naturally and quite properly pay closer attention to what Jesus said rather than to his method of delivery. It is nevertheless intriguing to note that the locations he chooses have regard to the practical considerations of acoustics and audibility in the open air. For example:

> Jesus began to teach by the lake. The crowd that gathered round him was so large that he got into a boat and sat in it out on the lake, while all the people were along the shore at the water's edge. He taught them many things by parables...[9]
> (Mark 4:1-2)

How interesting it is, in this context, to reflect that the greatest distance over which the human voice is audible, is not on land but across calm water. Jesus was evidently a very proficient proclaimer, technically as well as in other respects. In proclaiming, therefore, as in everything else, he is our perfect example.

Jesus' final command to his disciples was to 'go and make disciples of all nations', and to preach the same message he had preached to them. Not only did the message remain the same, but, for centuries, so did the medium. Thus we find John Wesley in the eighteenth century travelling the length and breadth of Britain on horseback, preaching with an unamplified voice to open-air crowds. Only with the inventions of the telegraph, microphone, loudspeaker, radio and telephone did the technology develop so that a message could reach beyond the range of the human voice. It is no coincidence that in the face of all these sophisticated resources, the formerly indispensable, seemingly indestructible town crier was virtually silenced, and brought to the very threshold of extinction.

But as we shall discover, in our own time town criers were to be reappraised, their talents re-appreciated and their age-old versatility rediscovered.

9. John Wesley preaching the Gospel at the market cross, Epworth

2
SHAKESPEARE GETS THE NEWS

How swiftly the news travels when 'this fell sergeant, death',[10] arrests a leading player on the world stage. Consider, for example, the deaths of President Kennedy, Elvis Presley, or Princess Diana. The announcement flashes around the globe almost instantaneously. The entire civilised world knows of such a death, and much of the attendant detail, within minutes of the final breath. It matters not how far away the death has happened; we have truly become a global village.

But news hasn't always raced on such swift heels. London's first recognisable newspaper, *The Corante*, was not published until 1621, five years after Shakespeare's death. He lived in a culture that was still predominantly oral as far as the transmission of news was concerned. Lending your ears to a proclaimer, to adapt his own phrase, was the key to hearing the latest developments. So, let us consider how Shakespeare would have heard one of the most significant national news bulletins of his lifetime. Return with me to the year 1603 . . .

Queen Elizabeth is on the throne. She is in her seventieth year and has reigned longer than any other monarch in English history. That she should ever cease to be our Queen is unimaginable, unthinkable, and unspeakable – literally. To speak of the succession has been declared a treasonable offence. Elizabeth has shrewdly observed that 'there are more that look, as it is said, to the rising than to the setting sun'[11]. She therefore refuses to create

10. Elizabeth I forbids anyone to speak of the succession

a rising sun by naming her successor – to the intense frustration of her counsellors – and forbids anyone even to mention the subject. But those same counsellors know that even Elizabeth is ultimately mortal, and secretly make plans to secure a smooth and uncontested succession.

Their motives are inevitably an amalgam of national and self interest. Ensuring a smooth succession will steer the nation clear of a bloody civil war, or of a foreign invasion in support of an overseas contender to the throne. Equally they are eager to manage the succession so that their own positions of power and patronage are at the very least maintained, and hopefully enhanced, under the new regime. The courtier Sir Roger Wilbraham echoes the thoughts of many when he notes in his diary that men were 'more hoping to be bettered by the succeeding king, in whose virtues and prudence there is admirable expectation'.[12]

King James VI of Scotland is identified as the preferred successor. A secret correspondence then springs up between Robert Cecil, Elizabeth's chief advisor, and George Nicholson, his agent in Scotland, who in turn communicates with the Scottish King. This is such a dangerous, potentially treasonable communication that the key participants are never identified by name but only by code numbers: Elizabeth is 24, James is 30 and Cecil is 10. By such covert means James is made ready to succeed to the English throne whenever Elizabeth should finally expire.

In March 1603 the Queen has entered what will prove to be her final decline. The preparations intensify. The entire apparatus of Elizabethan information technology is primed and ready to launch. From our modern perspective of mass communication it is fascinating to note that every element in the plan is engagingly human and alarmingly fragile.

Robert Carey, an ambitious and energetic courtier, recognising the rewards that may follow if he becomes the bearer of good news to 'the rising sun', has made elaborate, secret preparations to be exactly that. Fast horses are posted at ten-mile intervals from Richmond Palace, Surrey, where Elizabeth is fast fading, all the way to Holyrood, Edinburgh, where James awaits his invitation to assume the English throne. But it is pointless for Carey to set out without verification of the news of Elizabeth's demise. James had previously given a sapphire ring to the delightfully-named Lady Scrope, Carey's sister, on the understanding that it should be returned to him as a signal of Elizabeth's death. The instant that Elizabeth breathes her last, Carey leaps into the saddle. He pauses briefly beneath a casement window to catch the sapphire ring thrown to him by Lady Scrope who, as a lady-in-waiting, was one of the first to verify Elizabeth's death.

Carey then begins what appears to be an attempt on the land speed record. He leaves London on Thursday morning and is already in Doncaster that night, a ride of some 172 miles. He continues at a similar speed the next day, truly meriting the description 'hell for leather'. His diary recalls a setback on the third day:

> Very early on Saturday I took horse for Edinburgh, and came to Norham about twelve at noon, so that I might well have been with the King at supper time: But I got a great fall by the way, and my horse with one of his heels gave me a great blow on the head that made me shed much blood. It made me so weak that I was forced to ride a soft pace after, so that the King was newly gone to bed by the time that I knocked at the gate.[13]

Without pausing even to wipe away the blood, or perhaps thinking that the appearance of blood will add to the loyal-and-devoted-servant impression he is hoping to create, Carey is immediately ushered into the King's presence. He carries no official letter from the English court and James needs to be sure of this intelligence before acting upon it:

> ... he asked what letters I had from the Council. I told him none... yet I had brought him a blue ring from a fair lady, that I hoped would give him assurance of the truth that I had reported. He took it and looked upon it, and said, 'It is enough: I know by this you are a true messenger'.[14]

Only then are surgeons summoned to tend to Carey's wounds. For his pains he is appointed Gentleman of the Bedchamber (not the kind of reward I would have been hoping for). It has been a heroic journey which deserves to be better known. I wonder whether Carey's ride was the inspiration for lines soon to be written by Shakespeare in *Macbeth*:

> I have no spur
> To prick the sides of my intent, but only
> Vaulting ambition, which o'erleaps itself
> And falls.
> (Macbeth 1, vii) [15]

Meanwhile Robert Cecil personally takes responsibility for breaking the news in England's capital, using the fastest resources of Elizabethan information technology. The parchment scroll he has carried around for days simply needs to have the exact time and date of death inserted. The first official announcements of such critically important news in the heart of the capital evidently cannot be entrusted to the local crier. 'Mr Secretary Cecil' goes in person to a traditional place of proclamation, the High Cross in Cheapside, 'where were assembled the most parte of the English Princes, Peers, divers principal Prelates, and extraordinary and unexpected numbers of gallant Knights, and grave Gentlemen of note well mounted, besides the huge number of common persons'[16]. Thus with no means of amplification, the leading politician of his day proclaims the 'undoubted right' of James VI of Scotland to become 'our only lawful, lineal and rightful liege and Lord, James the First, King of England'. Cecil evidently displays the attributes of which any crier would be proud: a witness reports that he speaks 'most distinctly and audibly'. His vocal prowess clearly had the desired effect because 'at the end thereof [the crowd] with one consent cried aloud, "God save King James," being not a little glad to see their long feared danger so clearly prevented.'[17]

Church bells and bugles begin to echo the announcement. Riders are dispatched to every town and city in the kingdom with orders that the same proclamation should be made to their inhabitants. William Shakespeare, residing in London and drafting plays for the Globe Theatre, would almost certainly have heard the news in this way. There was simply no technology available to spread news other than a combination of rider, scroll and voice, prefaced by an attention-gaining handbell. What Shakespeare had recently written of Henry VI will now be equally true of James I: 'King of England shalt thou be proclaimed in every borough'.[18]

11. 'This news is mortal to the Queen, look down and see what death is doing.' (*The Winter's Tale:* III, iii)

In such a world, criers would have been more indispensable than we can fully appreciate. The town crier may now have been superseded by more efficient means of mass communication, but let us remember that for most of our history, almost every announcement, momentous or commonplace, would have been proclaimed from a scroll by the powerful larynx of a town crier.

Forasmuch as it has pleased Almighty God to call to his mercy out of the transitory life our Sovereign Lady, the High and Mighty Prince, Elizabeth late Queen of England, France and Ireland, by whose death and dissolution, the Imperial Crown of these two realms aforesaid are now absolutely and solely come to the High and Mighty Prince , James VI of Scotland, who is lineally and lawfully descended from the body of Margaret, daughter to the High and Renowned Prince, Henry the seventh king of England, France and Ireland . . . We therefore the Lords Spiritual and Temporal of this realm, being here assembled, united, and assisted with those of her late Majesty's Privy Council, and with great numbers of other principal gentlemen of quality in the kingdom, with the Lord Mayor, Aldermen and citizens of London, and a multitude of other good subjects and commons of this realm do now hereby with one voice and consent of tongue and heart, publish and proclaim, that the High and Mighty Prince, James VI King of Scotland is now by the death of our late sovereign, Queen of England of famous memory, become our only, lawful, lineal and rightful Liege James the first, King of England, France and Ireland, defender of the faith.

Cecil's proclamation, quoted in De Lisle, Leander, After Elizabeth; How James King of Scotland Won the Crown of England in 1603, Harper Collins, 2004

3
HEAR ALL ABOUT IT!

Nowadays you can go a whole lifetime without ever seeing a town crier. The only opportunities you have to encounter a crier are within one of the few places that have retained or revived this ancient office, on TV, or in a costume drama. For example, there is a particularly handsome crier to be seen, all-too-fleetingly, in Granada TV's film production of *Moll Flanders* (see chapter 17).

However, had you lived in pre-industrial Britain, a town crier would have been as familiar a sight on the streets as buskers, *Big Issue* sellers and traffic wardens are today. To put it another way, the town crier would have been as integral to your daily life as a newspaper is now. This analogy is precisely chosen because the historical town crier was effectively the forerunner of the newspaper.

In the days before newspapers you would depend on the town crier to inform you of news of every kind. In addition to news, a town crier 'published' the Lost and Found and Obituary notices, just as newspapers do today. Indeed the original meaning of 'publish' referred more to making public by crying aloud than to its later meaning of making public by printing.

So indispensable were proclaimers to spreading news and making public announcements, that in the seventeenth century a city like Chester had to employ four proclaimers to meet the need: the day bellman, the night bellman, the common bellman and the court crier. Just imagine how many cries they would make between them in the course of a lifetime. And then imagine that number repeated in every town and city across many centuries: millions upon millions of cries by thousands upon thousands of criers. Yet in nearly every case their proclamations have frustratingly disappeared into the ether, leaving not a trace behind.

However, there is an exception. The daily cries of one particular English town have been marvellously preserved. The town of Clare, in Suffolk, has retained a register of things cried in the market place by Clare criers, extending over 100 years (1612–1711). These cries give a unique and fascinating insight into everyday life in those days, and specifically into the daily duties of an historic town crier. No mention is made of the momentous events of history – invasions, battles or the deaths of monarchs – but instead the cries are about more everyday matters; cries, for example, on behalf of owners hoping to be reunited with runaway horses or runaway apprentices:

> 9 October 1692. Cryed one broune blacke horse Aboute 14 hands high, with a starr on his foorehed and whight slips on one of his nostrills, with one whight foot behinde, and a walle eye on the oft side, and the other eye is in his heade, but he is allmost blinde of both, and two sadle spots on etch side of this back, taken or strayed oute of the pastur of Mr John Brooke, minister of greate yeldom in Essex. [19]

One can only assume that the Pastor of Great Yeldham was motivated purely by love of his horse to pay the Clare crier to seek its return; a horse with one eye glazed over, and the other retracted, couldn't have been of great practical service to him. One wonders how it ever managed to wander away in the first place, or who would want to steal it. A blind thief perhaps.

The following cry about a runaway apprentice is particularly sad; even his frock and stockings were sad:

> 11 September 1701. Cryed in Clare markett, one Thomas Sparrow, apprentice to one John Barnard of Sudbury, who did Runn Away from his master on the 23rd day of last August; he hath a Ruddy Complection and broune hair, with A scarr upon his forehead, with a sad Cullered fuschon frock, and payer of Callimankoo britches, and sad cullered stockens. [20]

January y 31 1700 Cryed in Clare markett a Red Wilson
cloath with a blow frmye on it lost the 17th day of this
month lost betwene the markett streete in Clare & the
bottom of Mothergate the cloath of Richard willowes of
haudrill the tannour

Feb y 7th 1700 Cryed downe in Clare markett one Susanah
Datchwoule of haudrill the wife of Edward Datchwoule
of Kellmys Bumstod

march the 28th 1701 Cryed in Clare markett one John
wade the sonn of william wade of Clare glover that
non of the Kings subiects should lend the said John
wade Any thinge upon his fathers Account nor pay
him Any of his fathers debts

may y 23th 1701 Cryed in Clare markett a Gray camlott
Rideing hood lost this morning betwene long medford and
Clare the hood of m Robert Harris Cliff of Farrott of
Huntington sheer

June y 13th 1701 Cryed in Clare markett a little whight
Pigg About 5 weeks ould the Pigg of m John Harris
of Clare

July y 11th 1701 Cryed in Clare markett An ould bay
horse taken up att the Lordship att Rodywell

August y first 1701 Cryed in Clare markett fiue
weomtolls 3 of them Bull Calues A Black Bull Calfe
& a Redd Bull Calfe & A Brindled Bull Calfe and
2 Red cow Calues with A little whight one the
flanke on one of them taken up as Estrayes att
Pondiston Hall in Suff

September y 11th 1701 Cryed in Clare markett one Thomas
Sparrow Apprentice to one John Barnard of Sudbury who
did Runn Away from his master on the 23th day of last
August he hath A Ruddy complextion & browne hair
with A scarr upon his forehead with A sad Cullored
fustion frock & a payer of Callimanko britches & sad
Cullored Storkens

octob y 5th Cryed in Clare markett A Roone horse 13 hand high
with A Ball face with one eye oute & Aboute 8 years ould &
A gray horse 14 hand high & 4 years ould & both Bull tayls
& both trotters the horse of m malton of Wedmish thay
woar lost last munday night

octob y 5 Cryed in Clare markett A Black brown horse Aboute
13 hand high with A dott on his forehead 2 whight feet behind
& A Brush & tayle taken up last last Satturday by m Chodinke
Ware the lord of the manour of Stradgwoll

12. A page from *The Register of Clare Market Cries* which records cries made
between 1612 and 1711

One particular cry, from 31 May 1689, speaks of the age-old difficulties faced by husbands of over-spending wives, and reveals a solution no longer available today:

> Ther was Cried downe in Clare markett Catherine Frost, wife of Nathaniell Frost, of Hundon, in Suff., yeoman, by me, Edmund Warren.[21]

Ah! Those were the days of Merry England, when a man could have his wife professionally 'cried down'! Nathaniell Frost was by no means an isolated example of a seventeenth century man enlisting the support of a town crier, or bellman, to restrain his headstrong wife. Even after the lapse of three centuries, one can still sense the exasperation that drove a London clockmaker to this desperate measure:

> 13th April 1678 — Dyke of London, Clockmaker, desired leave of court to declorie his wife by the Bellman, she being a very idle and expensive person, running her husband in debt in several places. Leave granted. (Eastern Daily Express)[22]

How satisfying it must have been to have had your spendthrift spouse 'decloried by the Bellman' (i.e. don't trust her for credit) — so much more inventive, and entertaining, than simply cutting up her credit card.

A Dead Ringer

You wouldn't even want to die in those days without first securing the services of a bellman. In the days when urgent news could travel no faster than a man could carry it on horseback, news of an individual's death would spread more slowly than we can now imagine. If your lifelong friend, or close relative, lived in a village just a few miles distant from you, he could be dead and buried before you knew he was even feeling unwell. This would have happened on countless sad occasions the world over, but the following example has particular resonance.

In 1825 an American named Samuel had travelled to Washington, to work on a portrait he had been commissioned to paint. He wrote home to his wife, Lucretia, on 10 February saying, 'I long to hear from you'.[23] Tragically his longing was never satisfied because his wife had died at home in New Haven, Connecticut, three days earlier. He received a letter informing him of his wife's death on 11 February and returned home, travelling as fast as he could. But when he arrived his wife was already buried. Why is this example especially relevant to our story? Because Samuel's full name was Samuel Finley Breese Morse. If he had invented the electric telegraph a little sooner, he might have made it to his wife's bedside and been able to attend her funeral.

This story illustrates how important it was, in the days before electronic communication, to make provision in your will for the bellman to announce the news of your passing to friends and relatives. Otherwise, without the cry going forth from his lips, your own last breath, and burial, might be all over before any of your nearest and dearest got to hear about it.

In 1701, for example, Dudley Garencieres, the Rector of the Cheshire village of Waverton, stipulated in his will that:

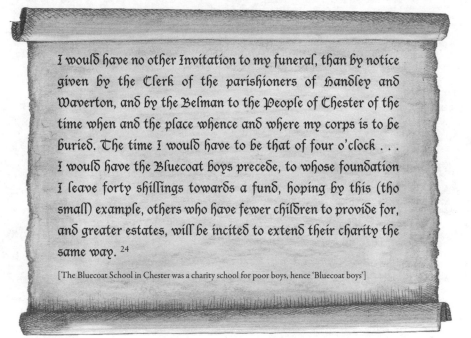

I would have no other Invitation to my funeral, than by notice given by the Clerk of the parishioners of Handley and Waverton, and by the Belman to the People of Chester of the time when and the place whence and where my corps is to be buried. The time I would have to be that of four o'clock . . . I would have the Bluecoat boys precede, to whose foundation I leave forty shillings towards a fund, hoping by this (tho small) example, others who have fewer children to provide for, and greater estates, will be incited to extend their charity the same way. [24]

[The Bluecoat School in Chester was a charity school for poor boys, hence 'Bluecoat boys']

Dudley Garencieres died in the same year he made his will. Little could he have imagined that, over three hundred years later, we would still be admiring the Christian generosity of his words. Equally surprising to him would be that our primary focus in recalling his funeral is a detail that to him must have been commonplace: the role played by the bellman.

13. A funeral procession in 1665, the Year of the Great Plague: 'the bellman goeth before'

James Hall, in his *History of Nantwich*, informs us that this role played by the bellman in summoning mourners to a funeral was called 'lating':

A very curious custom, commonly observed in the north of England and in Scotland in the eighteenth century, and known by the name of lating (i.e. inviting) was practised by the town crier of Nantwich in that previous century as noticed by John Ray in his 'Itineraries' under date Wednesday, 24th May, 1662, as follows:
'At Nantwich they have a Custom like that in Scotland: when anyone is dead, a Bellman goeth about the streets the Morning that the dead Person is to be buried tinkling a Bell he has in his hand, and now and then makes a Stand and invites the People to come to the Funeral at such an Hour.'[25]

42

Rival Reports

Another feature of a modern newspaper that the crier anticipated was the inadvertent 'publication' of occasional errors. I discovered the following item in *The Staffordshire Advertiser*, dated 26 June 1824. The story, under the headline 'Proclamation Extraordinary', illustrates how, in the nineteenth century, town criers and newspapers co-existed and still shared the duties of carrying news to the population:

> The Town Crier of Cheltenham being ordered last week to give notice, that all persons who do not pay their taxes on or before a certain day, should be exchequered, made the following announcement: 'Whoever do not pay their taxes before the 20th of June, shall be executed according to the law'.[26]

I wonder if we detect a certain glee in the new kid on the block – the newspaper – relishing an error made by the old hand – the town crier.

The Daily Post

Thus the historic town crier and bellman would have carried out most of the functions of a modern newspaper. In fact the very names of certain newspapers preserve the link between criers and the publications which would ultimately replace them, as we will soon discover. Prior to the development of printing, a crier would, after proclaiming, nail the wording of his cries, bearing the day's news, to some convenient wooden upright or post. By this means the literate minority could read the news for themselves, and read it aloud for those who couldn't.

Historical references to proclamations being made are plentiful, but accounts of who made the proclamation and in what manner are frustratingly rare. However, I have found one account of how a particular proclamation was made, detailing a specific instance of it afterwards being nailed to a post. In 1631 the authorities of Nantwich recognised that the forthcoming annual fair which traditionally attracted a 'great concourse of people' would be likely to bring into Nantwich the deadly plague which had already infected some other Cheshire towns. Therefore, to 'prevente the danger of infection', Viscount Cholmondley issued a proclamation to prohibit visitors from infected areas from entering Nantwich 'on the faire daye and foure dayes nexte after'. The wording of that proclamation has been preserved, but in the present context I am more interested in this account of the actual making of the proclamation, and the nailing of it to a post:

> Being 11 dayes before the faire, came into the open markett when it was at the highest, Venables [the bailiff] made soleme 'oyes, oyes,' sure on against [it] was done, John Offley did read the proclamation and Venables pronounced it with an audible and publique voice: then they walked all together to the cage where they did the like: and after fixed the proclamacion, wth some neales [nails] upon the cage poaste, where yt stoode for the space of four or five howers.[27]

The Cage was the place in seventeenth-century Nantwich where criminals were detained and proclamations read. It was situated in the market area, the natural gathering place where news would first be proclaimed and then discussed and savoured.[28]

This 'posting' of the news inspired the names chosen by many newspapers as they gradually began to replace the town crier as the chief means by which news was spread. This is why the current newspaper with the earliest origins, *Berrow's Worcester Journal*, founded in 1690, was originally entitled *The Worcester Postman*. Clearly *The Liverpool Daily Post*, *The Lancashire Post* and *The Yorkshire Post* have the same origin. Although Shakespeare never lived to read the first newspaper, he would readily have understood this new application of the word 'post'. In *The Winter's Tale* he has Hermione lamenting that she is 'on every post proclaimed a strumpet'.[29] This quotation also clearly demonstrates the close link between proclamation and publication. The accusation that Hermione is a strumpet (i.e. a prostitute) is evidently in the form of a parchment affixed to the post to be read by passers-by, but it is nevertheless referred to as having 'proclaimed' that news.

14. Nuneaton and Bedworth Town Crier Paul Gough studies the Chester competition draw which has been posted

Although it may seem strange to us today, even royal decrees, and the law of the land, would be issued by means of quill and ink, and spread throughout the kingdom by town criers and bellmen. Shakespeare captures this gradual dissemination of news in his play *King Henry IV, Part 1*, where he writes, 'proclaim'd at market-crosses, read in churches'.[30]

Until well into the reign of Elizabeth I, a royal proclamation carried the force of law. A memorable example of a royal decree publicised by a crying bell-ringer is to be found in the city of Chester, strategically located on the English side of the border with Wales. In 1403, after winning a particularly bloody battle against Welsh rebels led by Henry Percy, Henry IV decided upon measures to ensure there would be no repetition of a Welsh rebellion centred on Chester. All Welshmen were to be 'driven without the walls of the city . . . and no Welshman . . . remain within the walls of the said city, or enter the same before sunrise on any day, on any excuse, or tarry in the same after sunset, under pain of decapitation'. [31]

For these new measures to be effective the King's will had to be made known to the local population, and Henry was quite specific about the only effective means of doing this, commanding the Earl, Mayor, Sheriffs, and the Aldermen of the city, 'that you cause the articles of this brief, referring to the arresting of Welshmen in the city aforesaid and as to their not remaining in the same, to be proclaimed publicly in your bailiwick for the informing of the people'. [32]

The curious thing about this law is that it has never been repealed. Decapitation may appear to be a severe punishment for being a Welshman in the wrong place at the wrong time, but I imagine there was never a problem with repeat offenders. I hasten to add that modern-day Chester warmly welcomes its Welsh visitors. So it is only for fun that I have used the words of Henry IV's original letter to recreate the proclamation that Chester's town crier might have used in 1403:

Oyez! Oyez! Oyez!

In this fourth year of the reign of our
liege Lord King Henry IV,
It is hereby proclaimed, for the safe
custody of the City of Chester,
That no Welshman shall enter the walls
of the City before sunrise,
That no Welshman shall enter any wine
or beer tavern,
That no Welshman bear arms, save only
a knife for cutting his dinner,
That they hold no meetings or assemblies,
And that three Welshmen meet not
together, within the walls aforesaid,
under pain of decapitation.

God Save the King! [33]

4

WINE, WHISKY AND WIVES

People often suppose that the commercial and promotional work undertaken by present-day criers is a modern innovation. Nothing could be further from the truth. Advertising goods for sale, and acting as a public auctioneer, have been a feature of the crier's role throughout history.

We have already noted that in Ancient Rome the crier, or praeco, would cry out (i.e. advertise) the time and place of forthcoming auctions. At the auction itself the *praeco* also called out the bidding.

In his book, *History of Advertising*, Henry Sampson informs us that in twelfth-century France the public criers, or *crieurs publics*, were a regulated and established body, exclusively devoted to the advertising of wine:

> Public criers appear to have formed a well-organised body in France as early as the twelfth century... These criers of wine were a French peculiarity, of which we find no parallel in the history of England. They perambulated the streets of Paris in troops, each with a large measure of wine in his hand, from which to make the passers-by taste the wine they proclaimed... [34]

Unfortunately Sampson does not enlighten us as to why the French criers were so closely associated with the promotion of this one particular product. However, from my own experience as a crier, I can testify that wine is particularly efficacious as a laryngeal lubrication prior to crying, at intervals between cries, and when recovering from crying.

As Sampson correctly observes, there is no direct parallel amongst English criers with this French precedent. There is, though, a connection between English criers and a different fermented beverage which I feel duty-bound to record: the Ale Tasting Ceremony.

The office of ale taster (or *ale conner* or *ale founder*) was an appointment made by the ancient court leets – the manorial courts whose responsibilities included ensuring that proper trade practices were maintained in the selling of food and drink. The ale taster's duty was to examine the ale, and see to it that standards and proper measures were consistently maintained. Although the appointment of criers was also the responsibility of the court leet, I have found no evidence that criers ever assisted the ale tasters in their duties. But such is the modern crier's dedication to preserving tradition that many of them, including the author, have taken it upon themselves to perform 'Ye traditional ale tasting ceremony'. The local landlord is commanded to 'Bring forth a sample of your finest ale that I may drink and taste and judge its quality.' After conscientious tasting, which cannot be rushed, the anxious landlord is finally relieved to hear it loudly proclaimed: 'It hath a good head, a good colour, a good nose, and is fit for men to drink.'

The crier's role in historic ale tasting may be spurious, but English criers certainly did have a key role to play in the regulations of the buying and selling that took place in medieval markets and fairs. In medieval England all commerce was strictly controlled by the local merchants' guilds. Only goods made by local guild members could be sold within the towns. Any outsider attempting to trade was liable to arrest. This 'closed shop' was, however, suspended for a few days at annual or bi-annual fairs, if the right to hold such fairs had been granted to the town by royal charter. At the commencement of the fair it was the duty of the town crier to proclaim the suspension of the normal restrictions, and to announce the more relaxed regulations which would be applied for the duration of the fair.

Obviously the limitation of a crier's proclamation, then as now, is that it could not be cried continuously. The tradition arose that a glove was suspended from a pole at a high vantage point to remind all concerned that freedom from arrest applied for the duration of the fair. As long as the glove was up, any visiting merchant could sell his wares without let or hindrance.

The monopoly of the guilds has of course long been broken, but the tradition of annual glove fairs is still preserved in a number of towns in Devon. Every July in Honiton a golden glove is carried by the town crier on a pole garlanded with flowers. He proclaims the commencement of the fair with this traditional proclamation:

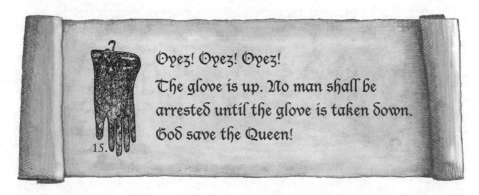

Oyez! Oyez! Oyez!
The glove is up. No man shall be arrested until the glove is taken down. God save the Queen!

15.

At some point in Chester's history the symbolic glove was crafted in wood. Samuel Lewis recorded the following:

Fourteen days before the commencement of each general fair a wooden hand as the emblem of traffic and bargain is suspended from the Pentice [the court building] adjoining St Peter's church where it remains during the fair a period of twenty nine days when non freemen are allowed to trade in the city. . . [35]

It was necessary that the people who resorted to these fairs should be clearly aware of the change in the laws for their duration, and proclamations by the crier were the primary means by which this was achieved. The wording used by Chester's crier survives:

Oyez! Oyez! Oyez!

The Worshipful the Sheriffs of this City do will and require and in his Majesty's name strictly charge and command all manner of Persons that shall resort to this Fair that they shall be of good behaviour and keep the peace as they and everyone of them shall answer the contrary at their utmost perils the Worshipful the Sheriffs of this City do will and require and in his Majesty's name strictly Charge and Command all manner of Persons that shall during this Fair Buy, Sell, Exchange, or otherwise depart with any Horse, Mare, Gelding, Filly or Colt that they and every one of them do make their repair to the said Sheriffs or to such person or persons as they shall appoint to record all such Contracts and pay such Toll for the same upon pain of such loss and punishment as is appointed by the Laws and Statutes of this Realm.

God Save the King
and the Worshipful the Sheriffs of this City.[36]

It is recorded that the sheriffs would pay the 'Cryer' 2s. 6d. each time he thus proclaimed the Fair.

The glove continued to be hung from the south-east corner of St Peter's Church, at the High Cross, at the commencement of every fair until 1836, accompanied by the same proclamation.

Thus we see that town crier proclamations have been an essential ingredient of buying and selling from Roman times through to the nineteenth century. It should come as little surprise, then, that one of the first celebrity endorsements used in advertising featured a noted proclaimer. William Childerhouse was the Bellman of Norwich from 1877 until 1905 and was probably the most celebrated bellman of his day. When Childerhouse needed false teeth, his dentist

16. Engraving of the High Cross and Bridge Street, Chester, in 1800, showing the glove suspended from St Peter's Church

took 'before and after' photographs of him which were printed in an advertising pamphlet.[37] The development of commercial printing, and the increased literacy necessary to read pamphlets and advertising hoardings, would in the long run do much to render this function of criers and bellmen obsolete. But before that happened, Childerhouse featured in this lovely instance of the old and new advertising media working together.

We will now consider an unusual and specific kind of auction, at which criers and bellmen were occasionally required to officiate. Anyone who has ever read Thomas Hardy's *The Mayor of Casterbridge* will recall the opening scene in which the down-on-his-luck labourer, Michael Henchard, enters the furmity tent in

17. A tight-lipped William Childerhouse, Bellman of Norwich (1877 – 1905) perhaps awaiting his new dentures

the company of his wife and child. After having his bowl of furmity (a broth of boiled wheat and spices) laced with alcohol, Henchard offers his wife up for sale and she is eventually sold to a sailor.

Although this scene appears in a work of fiction, such wife sales did take place from time to time, and when they did the local crier or bellman was often called upon to play the role of auctioneer. A surprising number of examples could be cited, but I have chosen to quote one in particular because it is reported with such flair:

The Annual Register for 1832 gave an account of a singular wife-sale which took place on 7 April in that year. Joseph Thomson, a farmer, had been married for three years without finding his happiness advanced, and he and his wife at length agreed to separate.

Thomson came into Carlisle with his wife, and by the bellman announced that he was about to sell her. At twelve o'clock at noon the sale commenced, in the presence of a large number of persons. Thomson placed his wife on a large oak chair, with a rope or halter of straw round her neck. He then spoke as follows:

Gentlemen, I have to offer to your notice my wife, Mary Anne Thomson, otherwise Williams, whom I mean to sell to the highest and fairest bidder. Gentlemen, it is her wish as well as mine to part for ever. She has been to me only a born serpent. I took her for my comfort, and the good of my home; but she became my tormentor, a domestic curse, a night invasion, and a daily devil. Gentlemen, I speak truth from my heart when I say—may God deliver us from troublesome wives and frolicsome women! Avoid them as you would a mad dog, a roaring lion, a loaded pistol, cholera morbus, Mount Etna, or any other pestilential thing in nature. Now I have shewn you the dark side of my wife, and told you her faults and failings, I will introduce the bright and sunny side of her, and explain her qualifications and goodness. She can read novels and milk cows. She can make butter and scold the maid; she can sing Moore's melodies, and plait her frills and caps; she cannot make rum, gin, or whisky, but she is a good judge of the quality from long experience in tasting them. I therefore offer her with all her perfections and imperfections, for the sum of fifty shillings.

After waiting about an hour, Thomson knocked down the lot to one Henry Mears, for twenty shillings and a Newfoundland dog; they then parted in perfect good temper – Mears and the woman going one way, Thomson and the dog another. [38]

Whether Henry Joseph Thomson subsequently found his 'happiness advanced' in his new relationship with the Newfoundland dog is unfortunately not recorded.

Earlier in this chapter we considered the part played by criers in promoting the sale of wine and beer. We will conclude this survey by considering the promotion of another fermented beverage: whisky.

An advertisement for Usher's Whisky appeared in 1911. Alongside an illustration of a nineteenth century bellman, it states:

> In the century which has intervened since the time-honoured figure of our worthy Bellman gave place to modern methods of advertising, the fame of Usher's Whisky has spread throughout the World. Though the announcements of the Bellman are now seldom, if ever heard...

The association between the bellman and the advertising of goods for sale, was evidently so established that when the role of bellman became redundant – superseded now by printed advertisements – it naturally occurred to Usher's Whisky to adopt the image of a bygone bellman as a symbol of traditional methods.

At that time – 1911 – Andrew Usher & Co was confidently proclaiming the demise of the bellman as an effective advertising medium. Now here we are, a century after the Usher's advert appeared, and criers and bellmen are back on the streets, called upon by local retailers and chain stores alike, whenever a novel approach to advertising is required. Today criers and bellmen are able to communicate to people in far greater numbers than our historic predecessors could ever have dreamed of. Their reach is no longer confined to that of the unamplified human voice – newspapers, radio and television together amplify and proclaim their cries to ever wider audiences. To paraphrase Mark Twain: the report of their demise was greatly exaggerated.

18. Chester's Town Criers perform 'Ye Olde Ale Tasting Ceremony' at the Coach House. The landlord, Neil Owens, is relieved to hear the happy verdict: 'We give thee this evergreen sprig to hang above thy door so that all wayfarers will know that thine ales are good.'

19. Andrew Usher & Co prematurely proclaims the demise of 'the old Town Crier'

5
WATCHMAN, WHAT OF THE NIGHT?

Samuel Pepys never set out to be an historian. That is undoubtedly why he often succeeds where historians fail. He records the kind of detail about everyday life that gives us an idea of what it was really like to live in those times. Hearing the cries of the bellman during the hours of darkness would have been one such normal occurrence:

> I sat up till the bell-man came by with his bell, just under my window as I was writing of this very line, and cried, 'Past one of the clock, and a cold, frosty, windy morning.' I then went to bed and left the wife and the maid a-washing still.
> (Samuel Pepys Diary, 1660) [39]

What a delightful picture of domestic bliss! Of course the most famous nightly utterance of the night bellman was 'All is well!' The cry 'All is well!' was not just a quaint olde worlde device to while away the time before late night television was invented. 'All is well!' carried reassurance and resonance when things at night could so easily, and for so many reasons, *not* be well.

In 1666 four-fifths of the City of London was destroyed by the Great Fire of London. Six years after making the above diary entry about the bellman's cry, Samuel Pepys went on to give us a vivid account of what it was like to be caught up in that momentous event. The ever-present dangers of fire, and the function of the night bellman, were inextricably linked, as we shall see.

The fire started in Thomas Farriner's bakehouse on Pudding Lane, and rapidly spread. Pre-industrial towns and cities seemed almost designed to optimise the spread of fire. The houses were constructed of highly combustible materials – wood and thatch – and tightly packed together. Overhanging upper storeys ('jetties') ensured that the houses were virtually touching one another. To make matters worse, the buildings were waterproofed with pitch which is itself combustible. And the fire brigade? – it didn't exist. Householders were legally required to keep leather buckets filled with water outside their homes in the summer months. Ladders, axes, and firehooks (to pull down burning thatch and timbers) were stored in parish churches. Larger cities also kept primitive fire 'engines', as immortalised by the children's rhyme:

> London's burning! London's burning!
> Fetch the engines! Fetch the engines!
> Fire fire! Fire fire!
> Pour on water! Pour on water!

But fire engines were of very limited use. There is a clue in the word 'fetch'. An engine that had to be fetched would probably not arrive on the scene until the fire had taken hold. It did carry its own tank of water, but once that was emptied it would have to be refilled from a local river, and the only means of doing this would be by buckets being passed along a human chain. Sometimes brass squirts (hand pumps) were also available. These too were minimally effective, and had themselves to be fetched.

Early detection of the outbreak of fire was therefore paramount. And that's where the night bellman came in. It was his duty to patrol the streets during the hours of curfew, vigilant to detect, amongst other things, any outbreak of fire. In that event, it would be his handbell and loud voice that would rouse the sleepers into action.

The very word 'curfew' has its origin in fire prevention. It derives from the Norman-French words *couvre* and *feu* ('cover' and 'fire'). It was essential that open-hearth fires should be extinguished, or at least covered, during the

20. A particularly elaborate example of a *couvre feu*

night when they would be unsupervised. Covering was achieved by placing a large metal cover over the fire, a *couvre feu*. By this means the fire would be starved of oxygen, but might still continue to give out some heat during the night, and could perhaps be re-ignited in the morning. The downside to this arrangement was, of course, that embers not fully extinguished, and unsupervised, might be the source of an outbreak of fire.

21. Seventeenth century fire fighters

The huge number of highly destructive fires that ravaged pre-industrial towns and cities is testimony to how often *couvre-feu* failed, and how inadequate leather fire buckets, squirts and fire hooks were to cope with the consequences.

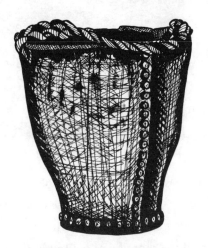

22. Leather bucket and brass squirt at the time of the Great Fire of London

That there weren't even more fires is undoubtedly due to the vigilance of the heroic, human smoke-detector: the night bellman.

If the night bellman was the nearest that highly-combustible buildings had to a fire detection system, the Great Fire of London did anticipate, in theory at least, the invention of a more sophisticated fire-fighting device.

The Lord Mayor of London at the time, Sir Thomas Bludworth, was roused from his bed to be advised of the fire when it was still in its early stages. Bleary-eyed perhaps, and in the heat of the moment – literally the heat of the moment – he is reputed to have dismissed the danger with this rash assessment: 'Pish! A woman might piss it out!'[40]

The poor fellow must have spent the rest of his life regretting those ill-considered words. Had Bludworth developed his remedy just a little further, he might now be remembered not for presiding over a fire disaster, but for inventing a fire *solution*: the sprinkler system. How cruel sometimes is the fine dividing line between incompetence and creative genius.

The Great Fire of London acted as a wake-up call. London was of necessity largely rebuilt, with some streets widened, and houses constructed of brick with tiled or slated roofs. Other towns and cities throughout the kingdom could not afford the wholesale demolition and rebuilding that the Great Fire brought about in London, but they did at least get serious about no longer permitting thatched roofs in built-up areas. In Chester, for example, the City Assembly (the forerunner of the City Council) resolved that houses within the city walls could no longer be roofed with thatch, but must be either tiled or slated. This they did at their meeting in January 1671. One might observe that this was some five years after the Great Fire, so they do not appear to have adopted this important measure with great urgency. Perhaps there were committees involved.

However, having finally reached this decision, the City Assembly had to decide how the new regulation could be conveyed to those who must obey it: the inhabitants of Chester. At this point we are still more than half a century before the establishment of Chester's first newspaper (*The Courant* in 1732), and a reliable postal service was even further into the future.

Another Chester bellman was therefore called into play, and provided the solution. The Minutes of the City Assembly record that this new regulation should be 'published throughout the City by the Bellman'.[41] Thus the day bellman joined forces with the night bellman in the cause of fire prevention in Chester. He did this by announcing the news using the only means available: loud cries throughout the city, prefaced by the attention-gaining ringing of his bell.

As Chester's current Town Crier and Bellman, I can testify that the efforts of my predecessors have been successful. As I walk the streets of present day Chester, I note that not a single roof within the city walls is thatched, as proclaimed by the seventeenth-century bellman.

The Minutes of the Chester City Assembly Book, dated 13 January 1671, have enabled me to reconstruct the cry that the bellman may have used to make known these new fire-safety regulations:

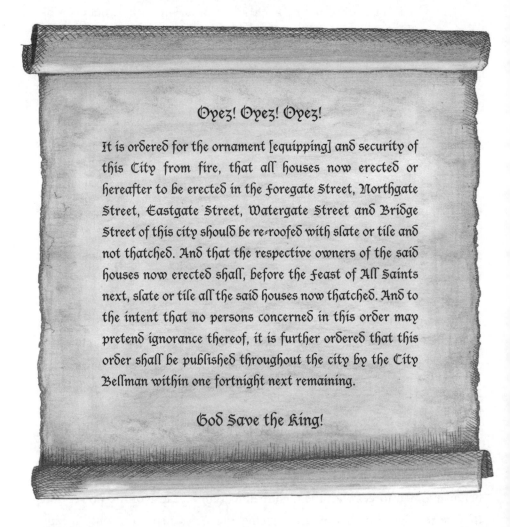

Oyez! Oyez! Oyez!

It is ordered for the ornament [equipping] and security of this City from fire, that all houses now erected or hereafter to be erected in the Foregate Street, Northgate Street, Eastgate Street, Watergate Street and Bridge Street of this city should be re-roofed with slate or tile and not thatched. And that the respective owners of the said houses now erected shall, before the Feast of All Saints next, slate or tile all the said houses now thatched. And to the intent that no persons concerned in this order may pretend ignorance thereof, it is further ordered that this order shall be published throughout the city by the City Bellman within one fortnight next remaining.

God Save the King!

More Thatch, More Fire

The Great Fire of London was the most famous, but by no means the only Great Fire. On 10 December 1583 the Great Fire of Nantwich, Cheshire, destroyed 150 buildings and made half of the town's population homeless. An

24. Firehooks in use during the Great Fire of Tiverton, 1583

eyewitness account tells us that the traditional efforts to put out the fire by a human chain, passing leather buckets of water, were disrupted by . . . bears! It seems that a local innkeeper, John Seckerston, kept four 'great beyres' for the traditional Tudor entertainment of bear-baiting. Anticipating that his inn would be consumed by the fire, he released the bears which seized the opportunity to bait the bucket-bearers, 'whereof the women were so affrayed they durst nott carrye water onelesse they were accompanyed wth men havyng wepons to Deffende theym ffrom the same beyres'.[42] What do you suppose that hostelry was called? It was, of course . . . the Bear Inn.

The Great Fire of Warwick, in 1694, demonstrates how quickly and easily fire took hold amidst wood and thatch, and the value of building with non-combustible materials. This fire evidently began as a kindling torch was being carried from one house to another. A stray spark from the torch drifted up to a thatched roof where it took light. A building in Sheep Street, where the leather fire buckets were stored, was one of the first to be consumed by the ensuing fire. Thereafter the fire spread largely unopposed. Dr William Johnson saw the fire beginning to travel down Jury Street towards his own home. To save it, he paid a group of men to pull down the house belonging to his near neighbour, Nathaniel Gistrop, who lived just two doors away in the direction of the approaching fire. He hoped thereby to create a fire-break and save his own property. However this action proved to be quite superfluous. The fire progressed half way along Jury Street until it reached Archer Mansion, which, unusually, was built of brick and slate. There the fire was halted. Johnson was subsequently sued for the demolition of Gistrop's home. You may smile at this point. I did.

One of the most famous buildings ever to have its thatch catch fire was the Globe Theatre. The Globe, where William Shakespeare was an actor, playwright and shareholder, had been built in 1599 in Southwark, opposite St Paul's Cathedral. It didn't require the vigilance of the night bellman to detect this fire since it happened in broad daylight in the sight of hundreds of playgoers. On 29 June 1613, during a performance of his play *Henry VIII*, the discharge of a cannon ignited the thatched roof. The building was quickly evacuated, without loss of life. One escaper had his breeches catch fire, but was saved when a resourceful fellow-playgoer improvised a fire extinguisher. Sir Henry Wotton has left us this account:

Certain cannons being shot off, some of the paper or other stuff wherewith one of them was stopped, did light on the thatch, where being thought at first but an idle smoke, and their eyes more attentive to the show, it kindled inwardly, and ran round like a train, consuming within less than an hour the whole house to the very ground. . . wherein yet nothing did perish but wood and straw, and a few forsaken cloaks, only one man had his breeches set on fire, that would perhaps have broiled him, if he had not, by the benefit of a provident wit, put it out with bottle ale.[43]

There is a neat modern twist to this tale. A replica of Shakespeare's Globe, completed in 1997, has been built not exactly on the same site but nearby. It is the first building in London to have a thatched roof since the banning of the same following the Great Fire of London in 1666.

25. The Night Bellman of London, 1608

If Any Base Lurker I Do Meet

We now begin to sense how great the responsibility of the night bellman was. His vigilance during the lonely hours of the night might be the only protection a town or city had against the outbreak of a hugely destructive fire. However his duties were not confined to those of a patrolling smoke alarm.

Imagine you are lying in your bed in Tudor England. The curfew bell has rung, you have dutifully covered your fire and retired to bed, being careful to ensure that the candle that lit your way bedward is fully extinguished. Rather than the comfort twenty-first-century folk derive from remembering that the deadlocks have been applied, and the alarm set, etc., you lie in the darkness only too aware of how vulnerable you are. The same factors which render your dwelling susceptible to fire – the flimsy wood and thatch construction – make you equally susceptible to thieves who may break in and steal. And if this does happen, there is no telephone by your bed to summon the police. Even if there were a telephone, there is no police force to call.

Will tonight be the night that your house goes up in flames, or that intruders break in and steal your life savings, perhaps doing you injury in the process? Every little sound is cause for alarm. Well, not quite every sound. Because it is this very array of potential dangers that causes you to welcome the way in which the night bellman punctuates the watches of the night with his cry of 'All is well!'

A centralised and uniformed police force was not created until 1829, when Sir Robert Peel's Police Act set up the Metropolitan Police Force. It would not be true, however, to suggest that previously the streets were entirely lawless. For centuries the streets at night were governed by the curfew, enforced by the Night Watch.

As we have seen, the curfew derived its name from the metal dome used to cover fires – the *couvre-feu* – but the regulations concerning safety at night soon extended to cover the times at which shops and taverns must close, outdoor lanterns were to be lit, the city gates were to be shut, and that no one should be out on the streets without good reason. The curfew was effectively: 'Lock your doors, candles out and time for bed!'

The enforcement of the curfew was the responsibility of the Night Watch, which was composed of a team of night watchmen supervised by the night bellman. To say that the night watchmen were less than highly trained, well equipped and highly motivated would be a huge understatement. They were generally recruited from the ranks of the old and infirm; those unable to secure any other form of gainful employment. In his depiction of Dogberry and Verges in *Much Ado About Nothing* Shakespeare comically suggests that the watchmen of his day might also have been known for a certain *mental* frailty. Dogberry appoints a watchman thus:

> *You are thought to be the most senseless and fit man for the constable of the watch; therefore bear you the lantern.*[44]

26. Constable Dogberry as depicted in an early 17th century illustration of *Much Ado About Nothing*

That the condition of the average watchman continued to be feeble is graphically illustrated by a report carried by the *Morning Herald* of 30 October 1802, which states that a man who applied for the job of watchman was turned down precisely because he was fit and strong. The Vestry (the local appointing body) was 'astonished at the impudence of such a great sturdy, strong fellow as you being so idle as to apply for a watchman's situation when you are capable of labour'.[45]

It is little wonder, then, that the watchmen sometimes failed to act as a serious deterrent. In between their hourly patrols they would take shelter in a 'watch box' (a small wooden shed like a sentry box). So little feared were these feeble watchmen that the hooligans of Regency London would make it their sport to find a watchman asleep in his box, turn the box upside down with him inside it, and leave him kicking his legs in the air and shouting until his fellows arrived to rescue him.

The inadequacy of the elderly and decrepit night watchman immediately prior to Sir Robert Peel's Police Act of 1829 is delightfully captured by this piece in *The Times* of 1827:

Had a council of thieves been consulted, the regulations of the Watch could not have been better contrived for their accommodation. The coats of the Watchmen are made as large and of as white cloth as possible, to enable the thieves to discern their approach at the greatest distance; and that there be no mistake, the lantern is added. They are fixed at stations, that thieves by knowing where they are, may infer where they are not, and do their best.[46]

27. 'Catching a Charley Napping' in Regency London

A balance has to be struck here. It was unfortunate that the bellman was given only the least able-bodied men to assist him in his duties on the nightshift. But a less than perfect Watch was obviously far better than leaving the streets entirely surrendered to knaves and villains. The night watchmen were not entirely unequipped for dealing with offences, carrying as they did rattles (to summon aid) and halberds (for protection). A halberd was a long-handled and fearsome weapon which was effectively a combination of axe-head and spear. The bellman, too, would shoulder a halberd and be instantly capable of raising the 'hue and cry' by means of his ever-ready handbell. Certainly William Shakespeare portrays the bellman's arrest as something to be feared. In his only direct reference to the bellman he personifies Death as 'the fatal bellman which gives the stern'st good-night.' (*Macbeth II*, ii) [47]

In this survey of the duties of the night bellman, from William the Conqueror to Robert Peel, I have generalised hugely. The procedures governing the enforcement of the curfew would have varied over time, and from place to place. The duties of the bellman in any specific place and at any point in time may usually be inferred only by brief references from incidental sources, such as the Samuel Pepys' diary entry with which we began.

Nevertheless some specific instructions to the bellman have survived. The Minutes for Chester City Assembly of 1503 record that the bellman was ordered to proclaim the following instruction:

Every man that hath been mayor or sheriff of the city of Chester, and also all innkeepers, as well they that have signs, as they that have no signs, shall have hanging at their dores a lanthorne [lantern] wyth candyll byrning in it, every nighte from that it be first night unto the oure of viii of the clocke, that is to wit from the fest [festival] of All Saints unto the fest of the Purification of our Lady the next following year. [48]

From all that has been said about the susceptibility of wood-and-thatch buildings to fire, it will be immediately appreciated that there is a curious irony here. City inhabitants were commanded to cover their fires at curfew, and have leather buckets of water standing outside their doors as fire prevention methods. At the same time, from All Saints (November 1) until the Purification of the Virgin Mary (February 2), innkeepers and prominent citizens were obliged to keep a lantern burning outside those same doors. This instruction is perhaps more understandable when we pause to consider that, in the days before street lighting, the streets would have been dark indeed, posing numerous hazards to those who walked them. Indeed two of Chester's main streets – Eastgate Street and Bridge Street – were paved for the very first time in 1503, the same year as the bellman's lanthorne proclamation.

There were variations in different places and at different times to the regulations concerning street illumination. Another bellman's cry, preserved in the British Museum, gives a similar instruction in verse, this time specifying the hours of six till nine:

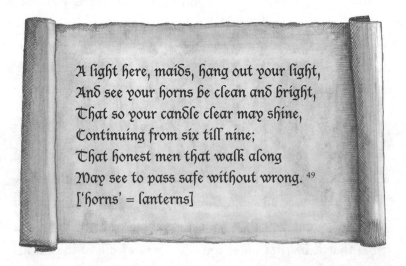

A light here, maids, hang out your light,
And see your horns be clean and bright,
That so your candle clear may shine,
Continuing from six till nine;
That honest men that walk along
May see to pass safe without wrong. [49]
['horns' = lanterns]

Casting the cries in self-penned rhyme seems to have been a common device of criers and bellmen, and one which is still emulated today. A charming extension of this practice was for the bellman to have a selection of his verses printed as a broadside (a one-sided sheet) and often illustrated by a woodcut of himself in his livery. These he would distribute to his 'customers' during the Christmas season as a timely reminder of the invaluable service he had tirelessly performed for them throughout the year. The reminder would hopefully spur the grateful citizens into bestowing on the bellman a pecuniary token of gratitude.

Most of their output has been lost, but one example is preserved in the Luttrell Collection of Broadsides in the British Museum. It is entitled *A Copy of Verses presented by Isaac Raggs, Bellman, to his Masters and Mistresses of Holbourn Division, in the Parish of St. Giles-in-the-Fields*, and dated 1683-4. The accompanying woodcut shows Isaac Raggs holding a halberd in one hand, and a bell in the other. A lantern hangs from his belt, and he is accompanied by a fearsome-looking dog. A dog appears to have been a common feature of the night bellman's arsenal of defences. The prologue neatly summarises the bellman's function as a burglar alarm:

Time, Master, calls your bellman to his task,
To see your doors and windows all are fast,
And that no villany or foul crime be done
To you or yours in absence of the sun.
If any base lurker I do meet,
In private alley or in open street,
You shall have warning by my timely call;
And so God bless you, and give rest to all.[50]

THE BELLMAN OF HOLBORN.

28. Isaac Raggs, the Bellman of Holborn in 1684

Bellman Wanted – Uniform Supplied

We have at least one job description for a night bellman which is historically and geographically specific. In 1649 an order was passed in Newbury, Berkshire, which said:

For the better preserving of the Town from danger of fire and many other great inconveniences that are likely to happen, and for the apprehension of all pilfering and suspicious persons, there should be a Bellman that walk the streets from 9 o'clock in the evening until 5 in the morning... and shout a distinct and audible noise to give notice as well of the present condition of the weather, as of the time of night, which Bellman is to have 5s. a week duly and truly paid by the inhabitants. [51]

Here we have confirmation of the two main functions of the Night Bellman. He would be required to 'preserve' sleeping citizens from the danger of fire and from the danger of theft ('pilfering persons'). When those two dangers were not present, his attention could then revert to the eternal preoccupation of a true Englishman; he would cry about the weather.

So, in his unassuming way, the bellman has, for many centuries and in every town and city, undertaken the functions of the smoke detector, the burglar alarm, the 999 call and the weather report. Who knows how many fires, even Great Fires, he has prevented? Who can tell how many muggings, thefts and murders he has deterred? Who can imagine how many times, in how many places, 'all was well' only because of his diligence? What an unsung hero the bellman is! The history books ignore him and not a single bellman is popularly remembered by name. Well, let it be loudly proclaimed that this book is here to put the record straight. Step forward the heroic Bellman! On behalf of countless citizens who slept peacefully and safely only because you diligently patrolled dark and dangerous streets, in all weathers, for their protection – and for just five shillings a week – Bellman of Britain, we salute you!

We are indebted to Nantwich historian James Hall for preserving this pen picture of a nineteenth-century bellman:

John Sutton was a well known character of the town. It was his practice nightly to watch the shops of those tradesmen who gave him a small pittance (10d usually) fortnightly, to try their doors, and plaintively cry 'parst ten, and a fine starry night' or otherwise, as the time and weather might be. After which he might be found in some corner or passage of the High Street, muffled up in a top-coat, and having fixed to his belt a bulls-eye lantern. In these retreats he was always ready to relate how many years it was since he had been in bed at night, or tell of the robberies he had prevented, and his once clever capturing a gang of thieves in Wall Lane; to offer a pinch of snuff, or slyly insinuate that he knew a place where they were brewing. He died at Christmas 1870, having been watchman for over 50 years.[52]

6

FOR WHOM THE BELL TOLLS

In previous chapters we have noted that the cries made by historic criers and bellmen were of importance in their day, but rarely of lasting significance. They had the kind of status that is commonly and literally dismissed as 'yesterday's news'. By day, criers would have reunited runaway horses or apprentices with their owners; by night, bellmen kept a watchful eye to detect curfew-breakers, fire and theft. Their duties were sufficiently important to keep them in full-time employment, but rarely of sufficient long-term importance to leave a permanent mark on the historical record. What Shakespeare said of a poor player might equally be said of a poor crier or a poor bellman – he 'struts and frets his hour upon the stage and then is heard no more'.[53] Each of his cries kissed local ears and swiftly died. The parchments on which the proclaimed words were written have, for the most part, long since perished. The handbells that prefaced the cries eventually cracked and were discarded, and the proclaimers themselves have returned to the dust from whence they came. Such was the fate of thousands of long-forgotten proclamations and long-forgotten proclaimers.

There is however a notable exception: the Bellman of St Sepulchre's. The cries made by this bellman were not of transient interest, but of 'deepest consequence'.[54] His exact words have survived, and live on. They were proclaimed unto condemned prisoners in Newgate Gaol on the evening prior to their execution, and also on the following morning when those prisoners were taken on their journey to the place of execution: Tyburn Hill.

29. Newgate, London, 1761

It is said that a light shines brightest in the darkness. To begin to understand the depth of the darkness experienced by those prisoners, we must first have some idea of just how grim a fate it was to find oneself in the notorious Newgate Gaol in seventeenth-century London. Conditions there were so horrific that three-quarters of the prisoners succumbed to fatal diseases before their execution dates. They were kept in unlit, unventilated cells with nowhere but the floors to sleep on. To add indignity to every other kind of misery, wealthy sensation-seekers would pay the gaoler (the 'turnkey') for the opportunity to view the condemned prisoners, like exhibits in a chamber of horrors. Little wonder then, that Newgate was synonymous with darkness. 'As black as Newgate's knocker' was a popular saying of the day, signifying that to go beyond that knocker was to enter a hell on earth.

On the day of the execution thousands would line the route from Newgate to Tyburn, a distance of over three miles, often pelting the condemned with clods of earth and other projectiles. A carnival atmosphere prevailed. Pies, sweetmeats and alcohol were on sale. Musicians entertained, and hawkers sold broadsheets of prisoners' confessions. Each prisoner was fettered for the journey, and rode in a wagon alongside, or sometimes sitting on, his own coffin. That journey was traditionally interrupted by a brief stop at an inn or tavern en route for the condemned to have a final drink of ale. There was no chance that one drink might turn into a second. After the first had been downed, the prisoner was put back on the wagon. Hence this is a possible origin of the expression 'on the wagon' meaning to stop drinking.

On arrival at Tyburn the miserable prisoner faced a gruesome death by hanging. As this was before the innovation of 'the drop', he would endure slow and painful strangulation, knowing that his last words or confession might quickly be printed up on a broadsheet simply to entertain the masses, and that his body might be sold to the College of Surgeons for dissection. Even the clothes worn by the condemned prisoner would be appropriated by the hangman whose perk it was to sell them. And let us remember that the crimes that merited execution were often comparatively minor.

30. The bellman at a hanging

It is against this backdrop of sustained misery, squalor and hopelessness that the Bellman of St Sepulchre's enters the story, bringing unexpected light into the darkness. St Sepulchre's Church stood opposite Newgate Gaol. From 1605 onwards, the St Sepulchre's Bellman was paid to proclaim to condemned prisoners that they should repent, so that they might enter into a happy resurrection. The exact words cried, and even the very handbell used by that bellman, have survived. The handbell is displayed inside St Sepulchre's, in a glass case at the north-east angle of the choir (see photograph on page 80). Here is the cry made on the eve of execution:

> All you that in the condemned hold do lie,
> Prepare you, for to-morrow you shall die.
> Watch all, and pray, the hour is drawing near,
> That you before the Almighty must appear.
> Examine well yourselves, in time repent,
> That you may not to eternal flames be sent.
> And when St Sepulchre's bell to-morrow tolls,
> The Lord above have mercy on your souls![55]

The origin of this tradition is also a story worth telling. Robert Dowe, 'Citizen and Merchant Taylor', might not be a household name, but he was evidently successful enough to accumulate wealth in his lifetime, and wise enough to make a forward investment of his wealth into eternity. Stow's *Survey of London* gives us the background:

Robert Dowe, Citizen and Merchant Taylor, of London, gave to the parish church of St Sepulchres, the sum of £50. That after the several sessions of London, when the prisoners remain in the gaole, as condemned men to death, expecting execution on the morning following: the clarke (that is, the parson) of the church should come in the night time, and like-wise early in the morning, to the window of the prison where they lye, and there ringing certain toles with a hand-bell, appointed for the purpose, he doth afterwards (in most Christian manner) put them in mind of their present condition, and ensuing execution, desiring them to be prepared therefore as they ought to be. When they are in the cart, and brought before the wall of the church, there he standeth ready with the same bell, and after certain toles rehearseth an appointed prayer, desiring all the people there present to pray for them.[56]

The bellman's prayer, to be 'rehearsed' (cried) the following morning, has also survived:

All good people, pray heartily unto God for these poor sinners, who are now going to their death, for whom this great bell doth toll.

You that are condemned to die, repent with lamentable tears; ask mercy of the Lord, for the salvation of your own souls, through the merits, death, and passion of Jesus Christ, who now sits at the right hand of God, to make intercession for as many of you as penitently return unto Him.

Lord have mercy upon you;

Christ have mercy upon you.

Lord have mercy upon you;

Christ have mercy upon you.[57]

It is not clear at this distance in time why the will specifies that this duty should be carried out by the 'clarke' (parson) but that all subsequent references have been to it being performed by a bellman. One possibility is that anyone who cried aloud after first ringing a handbell would inevitably be referred to as a crier or bellman. A second possibility is that the parson delegated the responsibility to one practised in the art of public proclamation; the local bellman. Whatever the explanation, William Dowe's bequest was carried out. We won't know, until we ourselves have heard the 'fatal bellman', just how many prisoners gave careful heed to the message of repentance cried by the Bellman of St Sepulchre's, stipulated in the will of William Dowe. But we can assume that, if they heeded the warning, they will spend all of eternity thanking him.

We do know, sadly, that not every prisoner who heard the Bellman of St Sepulchre's responded positively. One account of 1739 records:

The Night before Execution, it is customary for the Bellman to come to give Warning to the unhappy Persons who are to suffer, and when he had repeated what he had to say to them, one Albin who suffered, cry'd out of his Cell, God bless my Fellow Prisoners, and hang the Cryer. This plainly shews how stupid these unhappy Wretches are, altho' they are just on the Brink of Death.[58]

This is strikingly reminiscent of the two thieves who died on crosses at Calvary, either side of Jesus. One recognised his own sinfulness and called on Jesus to 'remember me when you come into your kingdom'. The other thief jeered.

We also note that the Bellman of St Sepulchre's is here referred to as 'the Cryer'. If people living alongside criers and bellmen on a daily basis used the terms interchangeably, you will understand why I have not attempted in this book to draw clear distinctions between the two roles.

It is interesting to note that Shakespeare's only explicit mention of a bellman occurs in *Macbeth*, and it is strikingly pertinent to this story of the Bellman of St Sepulchre's:

It was the owl that shriek'd, the fatal bellman,
Which gives the stern'st good-night.[59]

Just a few lines earlier we find these words:

The bell invites me.
Hear it not, Duncan; for it is a knell
That summons thee to Heaven or to Hell.[60]

The ringing of the bell, and the cry made by the Bellman of St Sepulchre's, were indeed a summons, or more accurately, an invitation, to Heaven.

Shakespeare wrote *Macbeth* in 1605, the same year as William Dowe's bequest. Shakespeare was then probably living in Silver Street, in Cripplegate, as a lodger of the Mountjoy family, less than half-a-mile's walk from St Sepulchre's Church and Newgate Gaol.[61] He must, therefore, have known about this unusual and solemn duty of the St Sepulchre's bellman, and probably heard the cry with his own ears. It is by no means fanciful to suppose that this was the inspiration for the above lines in *Macbeth*.

Before we take our leave of the St. Sepulchre's Bellman, there is another dimension to this story worthy of note. In addition to the normal ravages of time that devoured most seventeenth-century cries, and most seventeenth-century handbells, the handbell used by the St. Sepulchre's Bellman was itself so nearly devoured by one particular and famous disaster. In his brilliant book, *The Dreadful Judgement*, Neil Hanson tells how the Great Fire of London spared this particular bell whilst at the same time consuming others: 'St Sepulchre's lay almost downwind of Newgate . . . The tall tower topped with four pinnacles survived the blaze, but within it the wooden staging was consumed and the bells crashed to earth and melted . . . The only bell saved from the church was the small handbell.'[62] How apt that the handbell that was instrumental in saving souls from 'eternal flames' should itself be saved from flames whilst its fellows were consumed.

31. The handbell of St Sepulchre's

32. Thomas Turlis, Tyburn executioner in the 1760s

33. *Idle 'Prentice Executed at Tyburn* by William Hogarth, 1747, depicts a condemned man arriving at Tyburn travelling in a cart alongside his own coffin. In the foreground a woman sells broadsides of confessions.

7

THE APPAREL OFT PROCLAIMS THE MAN

"Pass me my wig and tights, dear, or I'll be late for work!" is my oft-repeated domestic cry. This might be an unusual request for a man to make of his wife, but then shouting at complete strangers on city streets is no ordinary job. Every aspect of the role runs counter to what is normal and everyday, and this includes wearing clothes that are more than two centuries out of fashion.

Town criers haven't always worn distinctive clothing though. One occasionally comes across black and white photos of early twentieth-century criers dressed in everyday clothing with only the handbell they carry suggesting their role. But for the most part town criers adopt distinguishing apparel, and carry various devices, to mark them out as people to be noticed and taken heed of. Shakespeare observed that 'the apparel oft proclaims the man'.[63] This is doubly true of a man who is at the same time a proclaimer.

Typically a town crier will sport a tricorne (three-cornered) or bicorne (two-cornered) hat, coachman's greatcoat with shoulder capes, a white shirt with lace cuffs, waistcoat, breeches, white hose and buckled shoes. The usual accessories are a handbell and scroll. Present day criers could choose any period of history for their dress. In practice the majority prefer the livery of a late eighteenth- or early nineteenth-century coachman. This Georgian or Regency style has become the stereotype of town crier apparel, and there are good reasons for this; this period was the heyday of criers, and a particularly elegant age of dress for men. The downside of the stereotype is that it fails to reflect the variety of apparel worn by criers through the ages. Before we look at these items in detail, let's briefly explore the concept of 'livery'.

34. The Victorian Mr Bumble, with Oliver Twist, wearing livery which harks back to the Georgian era

Anyone who has watched a film adaptation of *Oliver Twist* will have noticed that the Beadle wears clothing entirely out-of-keeping with the other characters. Whereas the latter wear the Victorian dress of their day, the Beadle often wears the aforementioned bicorne hat, greatcoat and buckled shoes – all characteristic of the earlier Georgian period. This reflects a tradition for local officials, or for domestic servants in a grand household, to be identified by wearing clothing which harked back to a previous period. The correct term here is 'livery' – a word denoting clothing worn to identify office or membership of a group, particularly household servants. 'Livery' therefore means much the same as uniform, except that 'livery' implies civil rather than military uniform. In common with military dress uniform, livery would emphasise decoration, especially on seams, cuffs, collars and fastenings. There was also a profusion of buttons. The buttons themselves would often bear a distinguishing emblem to identify the wearer as the holder of a specific office, or a servant of the particular household.

'Costume' is a word sometimes mistakenly used to describe a crier's apparel, but costume is more properly applied to theatrical productions when actors play a part. Criers therefore wear livery because they are not acting; they are the real deal!

So let's start at the top with the tricorne hat. The tricorne was popular in the late seventeenth and eighteenth centuries. Today it is the favoured headwear of mayors, town criers and Chelsea Pensioners. Traditionally made of felt, the tricorne would often be decorated with gimp (braid) and/or feathers, immediately offering great scope for flamboyance.

This was also, of course, an age when the wearing of wigs was fashionable for men. However not many town criers go so far in their quest for historical authenticity as to wear a wig. Let's not be too hard on them for this compromise. Imagine how it feels to be walking through a town centre in the height of summer, wearing a long-sleeved shirt, waistcoat, a greatcoat with shoulder capes, and a tricorne hat. You are already feeling uncomfortably hot and sticky. The last thing you want to do is add to the discomfort by stretching a tight-fitting wig across your already perspiring scalp. Historically wigs would have been made of horse, goat or human hair. A wig maker was known as a chiffonnier or peruker.

The coachman's greatcoat (pictured over), with its single or multiple capes, had its origins in tough practicality. The coachman would be seated up high and outside the enclosed carriage, exposed to the elements for hours on end. It was designed, therefore to keep him reasonably warm, with capes to encourage the rain to run off his shoulders rather than sink in and soak him. But today the greatcoat is perfectly adapted for the role of a town crier. The profusion of buttons and capes create the potential for an array of ornament and contrasting colour. And the romantic association with the golden age of coaching, and especially with highwaymen, is just perfect.

The alternative to the greatcoat is the frockcoat as worn by Thomas Roberts (pictured over), the town crier of Lichfield in 1822. The frockcoat is a lighter garment, more fitted to the waist, with a stand-up collar and without capes.

Beneath the frockcoat is worn a waistcoat, offering yet more opportunity for variety of colour and fabric. The shirt beneath that, by contrast, is always white, but doesn't miss out on ornamentation. Historically ruffles of linen would provide flamboyance at the wrists and neck opening. A stock would be worn around the shirt collar. This stock, also made of white linen, would have been tied in a bow and tucked inside the shirt neck opening. Nowadays criers often wear a bib of cascading lace, known as a jabot. The jabot, also worn by mayors, is actually a later misinterpretation of the ruffles sewn along the neck opening of the shirt,

35. Mr Harmsworth, the Town Crier of Basingstoke, 1905-1920

36. Thomas Roberts, Town Crier of Lichfield in 1822

37. Eighteenth century linen shirt with stock and jabot ruffles

but has persisted so long that it is unlikely to disappear. Similarly criers often wear lace cuffs, which would not have been affordable by their historical predecessors.

Next we come to the breeches. There's not a great deal to be said here except that criers aiming for authenticity should not, of course, have breeches fitted with a zip. Mine have the correct opening of a button-up flap (or was that too much information?). The legs from where the breeches end (just beneath the knees) down to the shoes are usually covered only by white hose, although the Lichfield crier is shown wearing black hose.

There are two options for footwear, buckled shoes or turn-top riding boots. Before we get into those, let me ask you, 'What is the term for a shoe or bootmaker?' Many people answer this question with 'cobbler', but you know, of course, that a cobbler is a shoe *repairer* not a shoe maker. The correct term is 'cordwainer'. This term has its origin in the word 'cordovan' which was a particularly-prized leather produced in the city of Cordova, in Spain. A craftsman who worked with cordovan leather therefore became known as a cordwainer. This is relevant because, if you are going to avoid the expedient of simply sticking a purely decorative buckle on top of a pair of readymade modern shoes, you will need the services of a cordwainer. Fortunately this craft survives today more than one might imagine, with craftsmen supplying footwear to the re-enactment fraternity, and other specialists making bespoke riding boots. In fact if you would like riding boots made by a bespoke bootmaker in London, they could set you back over £4,000.

Again, it all depends on how authentic you want to be. In the eighteenth and nineteenth century a cordwainer would make you a pair of shoes or boots by fashioning the leather around appropriately-sized wooden moulds called lasts. During this period boots and shoes were made on straight lasts, i.e. lasts that made no distinction between the left and right foot. You would then wear-in your new shoes or boots so that they gradually became adapted to your feet. Some purists do indeed go so far; I opt for comfort.

Buckled shoes are a common feature of 'crier attire'. Original eighteenth-century shoes would have had functional buckles, whereas most of today's

38. Eighteenth century shoes, turn top riding boots, and buckles

reproductions are purely decorative. Shoes need to be fastened once the feet are inside, and shoelaces were apparently quite a late invention. A possible date is 1790, but like most innovations they may have taken quite some time to become common. Before laces, the two side straps of leather (known as latchets) would be fastened together by a buckle, with sharp prongs holding the latchets in place. Very few shoes have survived from the eighteenth century, but the buckles were more durable and are often found by metal detector enthusiasts (though usually singly, rarely in pairs). My own buckles are historically accurate, forged from a cast taken from eighteenth-century originals.

Getting Attention

So now our town crier is fully clothed. But he isn't quite ready to make his proclamation. First he needs to get the people's attention. The most common association with a town crier is his use of a handbell as an attention-gaining device, but other devices with an historical precedent are equally acceptable. Scottish and French town criers often use a drum for this purpose, whereas Dutch criers may use a gong. A ram's horn (or *shofar*) was the biblical precedent, and is still occasionally used today. In fact the Ripon hornblower, carrying out a role very akin to that of the night bellman, famously uses a horn, continuing a tradition that allegedly dates back as early as AD866. A rattle, trumpet, bugle, posthorn and even a trencher (a serving vessel struck by a spoon) all have genuine historic precedents.

After the bell has been rung, or another device blown or beaten, it must be set aside to free up the hands to handle the scroll. The crier may perhaps lose a little dignity if he bends down to place the bell on the ground. Some criers, like Thomas Roberts (see illustration), wear for this purpose a 'baldric' slung over one shoulder and worn on the opposite hip. The bell is inverted into the baldric where it will sit silently until it is needed again. A baldric isn't just for handbells, it is literally 'a carrying thing', which explains why it was the perfect name for the general dogsbody, Baldrick, in the comedy series *Blackadder*.

Next we must consider the script to be proclaimed. Strict accuracy may be critically important if, for example, the cry offers goods for sale or is about a matter with legal implications. Relying on memory is, in such circumstances, entirely insufficient. Historically the words may have been written on parchment (scraped pigskin, goatskin or calfskin) with a quill pen, but the modern crier may perhaps be forgiven for using parchment-effect paper, which is more readily available. The parchment is then protected from the elements by being rolled up inside a leather scroll carrier, or perhaps neatly tucked into the front cleft in the tricorne hat.

The crier is now finally ready to hit the streets. He needs to take care though. He is probably feeling 'as proud as a toad with side pockets', to quote a delightful old Cheshire saying, and, if he hasn't compromised too much on authenticity, and has used high-quality fabrics, he will now be wearing some £2,000 to £3,000's worth of apparel.

So, dear reader, you need never again fear the arcane vocabulary of historical dress. Whether the conversations shifts to livery, gimp, greatcoat, jabot, cordwainer, latchets, trencher or baldric, you can now more than hold your own in any gathering of ardent re-enactors.

Now if you will excuse me, I need to put on my wig and tights, or I'll be late for work.

Attention Gaining Devices

39. Klaus Koper (Zandvoort, Holland): *gong* 40. Anne Hillebrand (Le Caylar, France): *drum* 41. The Public Crier of Edinburgh: *clapper* 42. Billy Clark (Nantucket, U.S.A.): *speaking horn* 43. Daniel Richer Dit La Flêche (Ottawa-Gatineau, Canada): *cookhouse triangle* 44. Henk van den Nieuwenhuizen (Oisterwiik, Holland); *'klepper'*
45. Robert Needham (Colchester): *rattle* 46. Alan Brown (Mossley): *bugle*
47. Rene Coupee (Almelo, Holland): *Alpine horn*

8

CRY ME A LADY

The role of town crier has usually been filled by men, but not always. We have already noted that a passage in Proverbs, dating back to 700 BC, specifically depicts a woman fulfilling this role, '*She* raises her voice in the public squares'.[64]

It could be argued that this woman is a personification of Wisdom, and is not therefore a specific person in a literal sense. Nevertheless female criers do appear in the historical record. Outstanding amongst these, for a host of reasons, is Beetty Dick of Dalkeith, Scotland. Thousands of her fellow eighteenth-century criers spent their working lives crying on a daily basis, but without leaving any record behind. Beetty Dick is the remarkable exception. We know so much about her. We know her dates (1693–1773), her address, her clothing (a linen garment, known as a mutch, which closely covered her head and fell down over her shoulders), and even her distinctive attention-gaining device: a trencher (serving vessel) which she struck with a spoon. We even know how much she charged to cry (one penny for each announcement), and the precise wording of one of her regular evening cries (see over).

We have two men to thank for preserving this wealth of information about Beetty Dick. Firstly her likeness was captured and preserved by the famous caricaturist, John Kay, as an etching. One of these etchings now hangs on a wall of my home, and is reproduced for you here. And her biographical sketch derives from a paper by Dalkeith local historian David R. Smith entitled *Characters of Dalkeith*. We are indeed fortunate that he has retained so much detail for us. He has kindly allowed me to reproduce this character sketch:

BEETTY DICK TOWN CRIER IN DALKEITH
BORN 1693 DIED 1773

48. Beetty Dick, engraving by John Kay, 1809

'Women were often employed in spreading the news of items that had been lost, the arrival of fresh food at the market or some piece of local intelligence. One such person was Beetty Dick of Dalkeith in Midlothian (1693–1773).

Beetty used a large wooden trencher that she hit with a spoon. The din was just about enough to stir the graveyard. The sound would rattle out at different places in the town, causing crowds to assemble to hear the latest announcement, for which Beetty charged a sum of one penny.

Every night she was employed to bawl out, "Tripe, piping hot, ready for supper the nicht at 8 o'clock at Jeanie McMillan's, head of North Wynd. Gang hame, bairns, and tell your folks about it."

Beetty never married. Initially she lived in the West Wynd (which became Eskdaill Street) and moved later to Tollbooth Close. She is buried in the east end of the Old Churchyard.'

Whereas it is true that town criers were usually men, it seems that Dalkeith took a pride in bucking the trend. The same writer, David R. Smith, goes on to list three immediate successors to Beetty Dick, all of whom were women. He also records for us the progression in the use of devices, from trencher to handbell to drum:

'Beetty Dick was succeeded by Peggy Haswell, and the clap gave way to the handbell as the means of rousing the townspeople eager for news. After Peggy, the bell went to Jessie Gervald, nicknamed "Gervald Gundy" on account of the gundy, a delicious sweetmeat manufactured by her.

Jessie was succeeded by Grizzie Brown, better known as "Bell Greasy", and she was the last to use a handbell in the capacity as Town Crier. The magistrates decided after her duties had ceased that a drum would be more dignified.

The Bell Wife gave way to the Town Drummer who turned out to be more expensive at eighteen pence for announcements.' [65]

When people hear that my wife, Julie, and I are both town criers, they immediately speculate that any arguments we might have must be noisy in the extreme. It's a reasonable assumption, but there was one barney between another husband-and-wife town crier partnership that must have been spectacularly loud, and it was the wife who evidently emerged victorious. Don't they always?

It happened in the Surrey town of Chertsey. Historically it was common for the role of town crier to be passed down from father to son, and so on through the generations. Henry Blaker had been town crier of Chertsey from 1895, until he was succeeded by his son, Albert Blaker, in 1906. It seems that the Blakers were devoted to family traditions as both Henry and Albert had also both been shoemakers, and three generations of Blakers served in the local church choir. But when war broke out in 1914, family tradition took an unexpected turn.

Albert Blaker was mobilised in the 6th Battalion of the East Surrey Regiment and eventually became a corporal, seeing service in India. His wife, Mary Ann Blaker, took over the position of Town Crier as a temporary measure. *The Surrey Herald* recorded that:

> *Attired in the picturesque Georgian uniform, which the townspeople purchased at the cost of, roughly, £30, Mrs Mary Ann Blaker commenced her duties as Town Crier on Tuesday 3rd November 1914.*[66]

It seems that Mary Ann took to the job immediately. According to one report, she was selling postcards of herself in her new role twenty-four hours after taking over. When her husband returned to Chertsey in 1918, having survived the war, she refused to relinquish the job.

She evidently became an active and prominent person in the town, leading processions on public holidays and announcing the results of elections. Local press coverage at the time claimed her to be 'England's first woman town crier'. Such claims are always hard to substantiate. Certainly her fame spread as far as Boston, USA, when she was featured in an edition of the *Christian Science Monitor*, as well as being the subject of a radio interview in England, in the days when such interviews were a rare privilege.

49. Mary Ann Blaker, Town Crier of Chertsey

Mary Ann Blaker died on 19 November 1940, aged 71. She therefore held on to this 'temporary' appointment for 26 years, and performed her last official duty just ten days before she passed away. It had been a 'stepping into the breach' of some duration. What Albert Blaker, the former town crier of Chertsey, had to say about his wife's career has, unfortunately, not been recorded. Perhaps she didn't permit him to comment.

Whereas female criers like Beetty Dick and Mary Ann Blaker were very much the exception historically, they are by no means a rarity nowadays. It isn't easy to say how many criers there are in Britain today, nor the exact proportion of those who are female. There are two organisations which British criers may join – the Ancient & Honourable Guild of Town Criers, and the Loyal Company of Town Criers – but not all criers register for membership of either organisation. As a rough estimate, there are probably in the region of 200 criers active in Britain today, and at least twenty-eight of these are female.

It's highly unlikely that the concept of attending a town criers' competition was one that was ever presented to Beetty Dick or to Mary Ann Blaker. Competitions are, however, very much part of the life of most contemporary criers. In such competitions, the women compete on equal terms with the men, and they wouldn't have it any other way.

My wife and I were privileged to compete in the 1997 World Town Crier Championship on Vancouver Island, Canada. At the Awards Banquet on the last evening I well remember the surprise, and delight, which greeted the news that a lady crier – the irrepressible Judy Campbell of Echuca-Moama, Australia – had been placed second. It had previously been so rare to see lady criers being placed in the big competitions.

The trend for male dominance continued however, despite this exception. Then in 2002, at our own Loyal Company of Town Criers British Championship, another lady was placed second – my wife, Julie Mitchell. But would a lady ever break through the glass ceiling and become a champion at one of the major national or international competitions? Well a lady *has* broken through. In May 2008 the Barnoldswick Town Crier, Eliza Mowe, became the new European Champion!

50. The author's favourite lady crier: Julie Mitchell, Town Crier of Chester

51. Betty Kading
(Orangeville, Ontario, Canada)

52. Eliza Mowe
(Barnoldswick, England)

53. Caroline Robinson
(Palmerston North, New Zealand)

54. Judy Campbell
(Echuca-Moama, Australia)

9

LAST OF THE CITY BELLMEN

Proudly displayed in gold lettering on fine oak panelling, in the Committee Room in Chester Town Hall, are the names of every person ever to have been Mayor of Chester (or *Lord* Mayor since the year 2,000). The first name heading this list is that of William the Clerk, who was the first known Mayor of Chester in 1238. The panels stretch across two entire walls and bear 629 names.

The office of Sheriff goes back even further. In fact Chester lays claim to being the first English town to have a sheriff. The first mention of a sheriff in Chester is in a charter to the Abbey of St Werbergh (c.1121), and the first sheriffs whose names we know were Adam the Vintner and Richard Bounz (1243–44); in the early years in Chester two sheriffs held the office simultaneously. The record of past sheriffs is likewise displayed in gold for all to see.

When I became Chester's Town Crier and Bellman I fondly imagined that I would similarly be able to trace the names and dates of my predecessors, for at least as far back as the mayors and sheriffs. The reality was disappointing. The record of town criers and bellmen in Chester is, as in other towns and cities, patchy and incomplete. These officials may have been an integral part of everyday life, but it seems that simply holding such roles was not sufficient to warrant their names being recorded for posterity. By and large town criers and bellmen have only tended to leave their mark on the historical record by doing something beyond simply discharging their everyday duties. They typically create a trace by, for example, getting involved in an affray or legal dispute, or by being granted payments for livery or equipment renewal. Thus, for example, we know that a certain Richard Woodcocke was Bellman of Chester in 1598 only because the Assembly Minutes record that he was granted 'a tymber mast typt at both ends and embellished in the middest with silver'.[67]

The earliest reference to a crier in Chester is in 1553 when the unnamed crier was paid 13d. for 'ridunge the Banes' for the Chester Mystery Plays. The Banes were short extracts which 'set forth the matter of the plays in brief'.[68] A bellman is first recorded in 1540 and that reference is, in contrast to later ones, helpfully detailed. Again the bellman is unnamed and again it is his fees that are recorded. These include attending burials – the fees for this are graded according to the financial status of the deceased – and for proclaiming lost items: 'When he goythe for anething that is loste, id [one penny].'

As we have already noted, proclamations were made in association with some of the most colourful moments in Chester's history – such as the proclamation against Welshmen within the city walls (1403), the proclamation of Charles I as a traitor (1646), and the proclamation forbidding thatched roofs within the city walls (1671) – but frustratingly on all these occasions the name of the crier or bellman making the proclamation has not been recorded. In contrast to the 629 meticulously recorded names of Chester mayors, we know the names of only 30 of Chester's historic criers and bellmen.

I have listed their names below with whatever date we have that ties them into the historical record. This might be the year of appointment, resignation, death, or some specific incident within their period in office.

1593 Thomas Richardson
1598 Richard Woodcock
1600 Henry Sterrington
1600 John Person
1607 George Tunnall
1632 Thomas Knowsley (died)
1632 Ralph Minshull
1662 Robert Moulson
1681 John Whitehead (day bellman)

1655 Mr Sutton
1663 Ralph Joynson (appointed night bellman)
1685 George Tunnall (bellman, died 1708)
1690 Ralph Leigh
1699 William Warmingham (crier)
1702 William Willoughby (became common crier)
1708 Thomas Booth (died 1715)
1711 John Beagh (died 1711, night bellman)
1711 William Wisnall (or Wiswall)
1715 John Fearnall Jnr
1719 Thomas Posnitt (died 1743)
1721 James Bateman (until 1734)
1743 John Posnitt
1792 William Ratcliffe (crier)
1792 John Yarwood (appointed day and night bellman)
1825 George Topham (resigned as crier, but reappointed the same month!)
1859 William Clarke
1863 George Musgrave
1869 John Secrie (died 1873)
1873 George Octavius Carter (resigned 1874)
1874 John Jeffery (resigned 1897)
    Appointment discontinued.
1978 Tom Clarkson (appointed 18 October)
1981 Mike Chittenden (appointed April)
1992 David Maguire (appointed 15 July)
1997 David Mitchell (appointed City Bellman 27 May)
1998 David and Julie Mitchell jointly appointed Town Criers of Chester
2008 Spencer Mitchell appointed Apprentice Town Crier of Chester (July)

It is only when we come to John Jeffery – prematurely dubbed 'last of the city bellmen' – that we have anything like a recognisable person emerging from the sparse records. We know more of his biographical detail than of all his predecessors put together.

Documents in the Chester City Record Office reveal that John Jeffery was born in Chester in 1818. Prior to becoming a bellman his previous employment included that of collector of market rents, chapel keeper, and railway inspector, as well as having had an attempt at running his own business which 'did not prosper'.

John Jeffery was appointed City Bellman on 30 March 1874. He was also required to act as porter to the Mayor when required. Jeffery is the only Chester Bellman of whom we have a photographic record, and a detailed description of his livery. We even have his notebook in which the wording of his proclamations is entered in an attractive copperplate hand. These include a context which may be unique to Chester, 'the 'Proclamation for starting the Horses on the Roo Dee' (the Roodee is the name of Chester's racecourse). It reads, 'Gentlemen are you all ready? Away and God speed yea!'

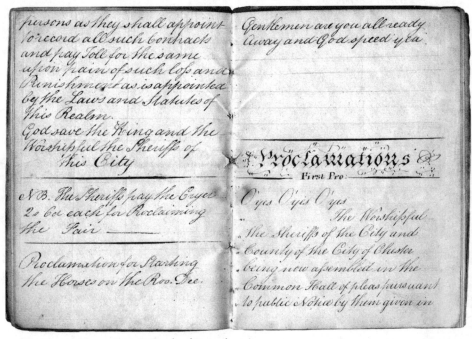

55. Chester Town Crier's 'Book of Precedents'

Whilst we may be grateful for this relative abundance of facts, they tell us little about his character or his daily routine as a bellman. They don't breathe life into him. But a poem that has come into my possession which gives us a day in the life of John Jeffery that is both vivid and intriguing. This particular day in John Jeffery's working life evidently begins quite typically – he encounters an American tourist on the streets of Chester – but becomes anything but typical when the mysterious stranger gradually reveals his true identity. Here is the poem:

56. John Jeffery, Bellman of Chester, 1874 – 1897

Old Jeffery, the City Crier

Old Chester City may well boast
A Crier of renown;
Who takes a most important part
In matters of the town;
Each grand procession with the Mayor
He always leads the van,
Mayor, Alderman and Councillor
Respect the old Bellman.

To see him in his best array,
Gold braided vest and coat;
The citizens do truly say
He is a man of note.
He rings his bell in measured time,
Each note distinct and clear;
And when he cries, no one denies
He makes the people hear.

One day, when busy in his shop
This worthy city Crier,
A stranger came, with hurried steps
His services to hire.
My friend said he, I've lost a dog,
A famous black and tan,
And to recover which, I'm told
You are the very man.

The broad Atlantic I have crossed
Direct from Yankee land,
And how I came to lose my dog

57.

102

I do not understand;
But quick, my friend, what is your charge
For crying through the town?
When Jeffery told him one and six,
He threw him half a crown.

Old Jeff was taken by surprise
The stranger being so free,
For he admits he seldom gets
A shilling o'er his fee,
So he determined there and then
To hunt the City round,
And forage out the stranger's dog,
That's if it could be found.

He soon put on his coat and cap,
His work he threw aside,
For to oblige his customers
He always took a pride;
With bell in hand he soon set out,
The stranger kept behind
To see old Jeffery ring his bell
The precious dog to find.

One bolted from a butcher's shop,
When they were in the street,
Some boys gave chase, for in his mouth
He had a piece of meat;
Old Jeff was soon upon his track,
And eyed him as he ran,
It proved to be a black and white
Instead of black and tan.

He rang his bell and oft proclaimed
About a dog being lost,
The owner wished to get it back,
No matter what it cost;
From street to street he trudged his way,
Each stray dog he would scan,
But all in vain, he missed to find
The famous black and tan.

The stranger feeling satisfied
That Jeff had done his best
He cordially invited him
To go and take a rest;
So they agreed to get a glass
Of Barlow's noted beer,
The Coach and Horses, Northgate Street
To where they both did steer

58. The Coach and Horses, Northgate Street

Now Jeffery, being a man of sense,
And liked a social chat,
He full entertained his friend
While in The Coach they sat;
Says Jeffery, 'Ere you go away

And leave me with my bell,
What part of the far western shore
Is it where you do dwell?'

'Astoria's where I make my home,'
The stranger said quite clear,
'Where I have left till my return
A wife and children dear;
And when I get back to them,
'Twill be my heart's desire
To tell them my adventure with
Old Chester City Crier.

The town that I have mentioned is
A noted place for fish,
'Tis quite a common thing to see
A salmon on a dish;
The rivers lined with fishing boats,
And salmon caught in scores,
Which are preserved in canisters,
And sent to other shores.'

"'Tis strange said Jeff, for I've a son
Who lives in that same place,
And many years have passed away
Since I have seen his face;
He keeps a large establishment;
I hear he's quite a nob,
His name is Robert Jeffery, but
I always called him Bob.'

'I know your son quite well, old friend,
And saw him every day;

I got these smokes from his abode
Before I came away;
He keeps a noted restaurant,
His name's known far and wide,
And those who patronise his place
Are always well supplied.

Take this cigar, my dear old friend,
The flavour you'll enjoy,
And be assured in what I say,
It's from your long lost boy;'
When Jeffery took the precious smoke,
His heart with joy did throb
To think the stranger sitting there
Should know his poor Bob.

Now Jeff decided o'er that smoke
To lay his bell aside,
And show the stranger all he could
By acting City Guide;
He took him round from place to place,
Reviewed the Rows and Stalls,
The old cathedral they went through,
And round the city walls.

'Your kindness has been true, old friend,
And 'ere we say good day,
Just come with me to the hotel
Where I at present stay;'
They soon were landed in a room
Upstairs in the hotel;
Inviting Jeff to take a drink
The stranger rang the bell.

But 'ere old Jeff had touched his glass
He scarcely had a doubt
From what he saw before him there
He'd found the mystery out,
A name familiar on the box,
O'er which he quickly ran
Convinced him very forcibly
The stranger was his son.

Then turning round with anxious gaze,
Subduing hard a sob,
With trembling accent he exclaimed
Is it my poor Bob?
It is, cried Bob, with quick embrace,
And then with mingled tears,
The son and father had not met
For two and twenty years.

John Roberts
King Street, Chester. December 1887.

This poem was passed on to me by Chester City Tour Guide, Tom Hand. All that is currently known about its origin is that the author, John Roberts, was a contemporary and possibly a relative of 'Old Jeffery', the Chester Bellman.

We don't know to what extent the poem was inspired by real events, but I have seen surviving correspondence which confirms that members of the Jeffery family did indeed emigrate to the north west of the United States. They maintained contact by letter, and by a twelve-day sea voyage from America to England which a certain Robert Lambeth Jeffery made in 1887, the very same year in which the poem was written. He appears to be the inspiration for 'poor Bob'.

The poem supports our earlier observation that making lost-and-found announcements was a frequent duty of a town crier or bellman. In fact his photograph depicts him holding a 'lost' notice. This is a very common feature in portraits of Victorian town criers and bellmen. Furthermore the poem uses the terms 'crier' and 'bellman' interchangeably, which confirms that for much of our history there was little real distinction between the two roles.

John Jeffery held the office of Chester Bellman for twenty-three years, until failing health caused him to resign in 1897, at the age of 79. In his letter of resignation he cites the 'increasing infirmities of age, deafness, partial blindness, etcetera.' He died in December 1903 and was at that time described as the 'last of the City's bellmen'.

In 1903 it was quite reasonable to have supposed that John Jeffery would indeed prove to be the 'last of the City's bellmen'. No one could have foreseen the tourism-inspired bell-ringer revival which happened in Chester and elsewhere in the latter half of the twentieth century. The post of town crier was revived in Chester in 1978, when Tom Clarkson was appointed. I was appointed Chester City Bellman in 1997, exactly 100 years after John Jeffery's resignation, and Julie and I jointly became Chester's Town Criers in 1998.

There are two further links between John Jeffery and myself, the current Town Crier and Bellman. Prior to becoming City Bellman, John Jeffery had been chapel keeper at Queen Street Chapel between 1865 and 1873, the same church in which Julie and I were married on 5 August 1989, and the day my own career as a town crier began (see Chapter 10).

Finally the poem names the Coach and Horses in Northgate Street as the hostelry to which they repaired for a drink. This is the same hostelry to which, coincidentally, I would take a certain Darren Johnson to plan his public marriage proposal (see Chapter 15).

CHESTER'S TOURISM REVIVAL TOWN CRIERS
59. Tom Clarkson 60. Mike Chittenden 61. David Maguire 62. David Mitchell
63. Julie Mitchell 64. Spencer Mitchell, Apprentice 65. David, Julie and Spencer
Mitchell

PART 2
THE PERSONAL HISTORY

10

HOW DID YOU GET INTO IT?

'How did you get into it in the first place?' is by far the most frequent question I am asked. 'Providence!' is the short answer. For the expanded version please read on.

When Julie and I were planning our wedding – some twenty years ago – we were mindful of the weddings we had ourselves attended. We recalled the familiar dash to reach the unfamiliar church in the unfamiliar location before the bride got there before us. How we were rewarded for this success only by a rear view of the couple throughout the service. How the ceremony itself ended with a brief glimpse of the departing newly-weds as they made their exits. How the couple would be immediately kidnapped by a zealous and demanding photographer and be whisked away for an extensive, private photoshoot at a secret location.

Those of us not privy to this exclusive threesome would make our way along more unfamiliar roads to the reception venue, where we would languish in itchy formal wear trying to make a single glass of sherry last for hours, earnestly hoping that the celebration we had travelled so far to attend would eventually be resumed, hopefully in the presence of the bride and groom.

Having endured several such weddings, we resolved to give our family and friends a different experience. We wanted the event to be fun for them, not for the photographer. A theme was what we needed, and if the historic city of Chester was to be the backdrop, then history, we decided, should be the theme.

The invitations set the tone. As Julie is an artist and I am a calligrapher, we decided to design our own invitations. When the recipients opened the parchment-effect card, an armour-clad knight and his lady popped up to stand together before a medieval altar. The wording revealed that guests were invited not to a wedding but to a 'plighting of troths'.

Having thus raised expectations, we had then to fill in the detail. We discovered that when the *Book of Common Prayer* is updated, previous versions remain valid and may be chosen in preference to the modernised wording. We asked the pastor who was to perform our ceremony if he would be willing to go all the way back to Cranmer's original wording of 1549. He surveyed the Tudor language, full of 'thees', 'thous' and 'troth plighting' – neatly echoing the wording of the invitations – and declared, 'Well, I'd need a new pair of dentures to pronounce some of this, but if it's what you want, I will do it.'

67. The invitations set the tone

The bride's transport to the church was then booked to continue the historical theme: a horsedrawn landau with two smartly-dressed grooms in attendance. The form of transport for the guests from the church to the reception was less obvious, but eventually inspired another historical element. We discovered that the two venues were linked by the canal. A treat from a bygone era was therefore arranged for the guests. On leaving the church they would be led to the nearby towpath where a specially-commissioned horsedrawn barge would be waiting to depart.

It seemed that all was eventually in place. But for the day to get off to a good start, the bride-to-be had to be up early for her appointment with the hairdresser. She needed an early morning wake-up call, and when I chanced upon Chester's then-town crier, Mike Chittenden, I knew that he would be the perfect person to provide it. Unbeknown to Julie, I asked Mike if I could hire him to wake my bride on the morning of her wedding. He agreed to do so.

I was delighted with the arrangement. But then, just a week before the wedding, I got a call from Mike. Full of apologies he revealed that he had inadvertently double booked. When he should be waking my bride in Chester, he explained, he would actually be in Hastings competing in a town crier competition. He couldn't be in two places at once, and would therefore have to 'cry off'.

68. The Bride gets into her carriage outside Queen Street Chapel

69. A horsedrawn barge prepares to carry guests from the chapel to the reception venue

I was so disappointed. By now I had got my heart set on the plan, and had no idea where I might find another town crier. After giving it some thought, I eventually called him back: 'Mike, I wonder if you have got a spare outfit and a spare bell that I could hire from you and do the wake-up call myself? Obviously it wouldn't be as good as you doing it, but at least it would still happen.'

'By all means!' came the reply. Thus it was that, early on the Saturday morning in August 1989, I stood beneath the bride's bedroom window, clad in borrowed robes. I stepped into the breach – and into the breeches – and made my debut as a town crier, proclaiming:

> 'Arise fair maiden! Cast off thy slumbers and clad thyself in fair raiment!'

Now this is just between you and me, because my wife doesn't like me to say this, but for me this proved to be the highlight of the whole day.

All the neighbours had been tipped off in advance, and the whole street turned out to watch and enjoy. It was indeed the perfect start to the day. But it wasn't immediately evident just how consequential the Chester Crier's diary confusion would prove to be. Some three years later Mike relinquished his post just as I was feeling the need for a career change. Ordinarily it would never have occurred to me to want to become a town crier, but inspired by my wedding day debut, I applied for the job. Following interviews and auditions, I was appointed Deputy Town Crier of Chester in 1992, and then in 1998 Julie and I jointly became Town Criers of Chester. The rest, as they say, is history, or rather, the re-enactment of history.

'There is Providence in the fall of a sparrow',[69] said Hamlet. There's Providence, too, in the double booking of a town crier.

11
IT'S A CRIER'S LIFE FOR ME!

Present-day British town criers go to great lengths to follow in the footsteps of their historic predecessors. We invest in bespoke clothing to replicate the dress worn by criers of bygone days, particularly favouring eighteenth-century styles. We invariably begin a proclamation with three cries of 'Oyez!' and we rigorously preserve the traditional town crier's loyalty to the reigning monarch by concluding with 'God Save the Queen!'

There are, however, limits to our striving for authenticity. Patrolling the dark and dangerous streets at night, in all weathers, with little more than a handbell for protection, is a precedent which no modern-day crier seeks to maintain. The same could be said of working eight-hour shifts for five shillings a week. In fact the working life of a contemporary crier is in many respects 'a far cry' from that of his ancestors. Nowadays we are favoured with short shifts, in daylight, and often in sunshine. And generally speaking we can command fees somewhat in excess of five shillings.

There would have been a strict routine to the hours, duties and daily round of the historic town crier. The outstanding attraction of the modern role for me is its sheer variety. No two days are ever the same. In a typical month my assignments might include: promoting a new store, delivering a criergram (the good taste alternative to the stripagram), opening a show home, officiating at a golden wedding celebration, leading a parade, making a public marriage proposal, acting as Master of Ceremonies at a dinner, filming for television, and waking a bride on the morning of her wedding. There is also seasonal variety. In summer I open fetes and launch helium-filled balloons; in winter I switch on Christmas lights, lead Santa parades and make after dinner speeches.

Some of the rarer assignments include leaping off the tower of a Chester city centre church on a zip wire alongside a radio presenter, appearing in a feature film (*24 Hour Party People* with Steve Coogan), rolling cheeses down Chester's Bridge Street, and making a wedding proclamation on horseback (see Chapter 16). What other job could offer such variety?

High Noon at the High Cross

70. The High, Chester, prior to the Civil War, with images of saints in the niches, and surmounted by orb and cross

In the midst of all this modern-day variety, there is also, in Chester, the continuation of a long tradition. Other places have town criers, but only Chester retains the tradition of regular proclamations at a fixed time and place. Proclamations have been made at the High Cross since the Middle Ages. In fact the High Cross could almost have been designed for the purpose of public proclamations.

The street plan of modern Chester still follows the layout of the Roman fortress founded in AD79 (*chester* in Latin means camp), with all four main streets radiating out from a central hub: the High Cross. There is a second crossroads lower down Eastgate Street, so the central crossroads, occupying the higher elevation, is known as the High Cross.

The High Cross is a cross in a second sense of the word in that a sandstone structure had stood at this point since the fourteenth century (the first recorded mention being in 1377). This structure was originally gilded and surmounted by an orb and cross. Following the Great Siege of Chester during the Civil War, the Parliamentarians eventually captured the city in 1646. One of their first actions was to smash the sandstone cross at the High Cross, because it contained images of saints in niches near the pinnacle and was therefore regarded by the Puritan-Parliamentarians as idolatrous. From the place where it had stood, King Charles I was proclaimed a traitor. This was, of course, the seventeenth-century equivalent of victorious invading forces seizing control of the media and immediately broadcasting 'regime change'.

The broken sections of the cross were wonderfully preserved. For many years they were stored in the adjacent Church of St Peter. In 1975 the sandstone cross, comprising both original and new sections, was reassembled close to the original position at the High Cross. However, the cross surmounting the orb, and figures of saints, have not been restored. History has now come full circle because Chester's town criers make their midday proclamations standing on the base of the cross, always concluding with 'God save the Queen!' Hardly what Oliver Cromwell had in mind.

71. The High Cross today

In the days when the punishment of wrong-doers was a good deal more public and colourful than it is today, the High Cross was the site of the stocks, the pillory and the whipping post. Hangings have taken place here, marriage banns proclaimed, and labourers hired.

In the eighteenth century sedan chair carriers would 'park' their chairs at the High Cross waiting for customers in the same way that taxis now wait in taxi ranks. It has also been the site of bull- and bear-baiting. These popular 'entertainments' could be messy affairs. On one particular occasion the Town Crier of Chester proclaimed this advice to on-lookers, 'Oyez! Oyez! Oyez! If any man stand within twenty yards of the bullring, let him take what comes!'[70]

Little wonder, then, that one writer has said, 'At the Cross we are upon ground hallowed by as long a succession of civic incidents as any spot in our kingdom.'[71]

So why is it the perfect place to proclaim? The High Cross is surrounded by tall, historic buildings, mostly built during the Victorian era but in imitation-Tudor style. These buildings provide not only a very apt historic backdrop to this antiquated means of communication, but also acoustic 'bounce' for the crier's voice. In addition the pedestrianisation of the area which took place in the 1970s affords ample space for the tourists to watch and listen in safety.

The final dimension of proclamation-perfection is provided by the world-famous Chester Rows, two-tiered shopping galleries dating back to the Middle Ages. These afford an advantageous vantage point from which to watch and listen, and shelter on those (exceedingly rare) summer days when it rains. On such occasions the tourists can stay dry, and enjoy watching the crier get wet on their behalf.

72. A visitor from the Colonies detained in the stocks at the High Cross

You will be pleased to know that, as Chester's current town crier, I have revived the tradition of imprisoning folk in the stocks. I would be pleased to detain you in this manner at your earliest convenience. You would however have to bring your own rotten fruit because we have nothing but the finest, fresh produce here in Chester.

A crowd of 200 or so people from all around the world regularly gather for the midday proclamation, and of course most are equipped with cameras. I imagine that it is for this very reason that Chester City Council chose two exceptionally good-looking people to be their modern-day proclaimers. However, I must add that, at the time of going to press, the Council is yet to confirm this supposition.

73. The midday proclamation at the High Cross, Chester

Cries for a Prize

Another dimension to the modern role which would have been undreamt of by our predecessors is the opportunity to take part in town crier competitions. In the summer month criers may get invited to as many as a dozen competitions in various locations around the country. Host venues are happy to put on a town crier competition because it creates colour, spectacle and entertainment. A competition will also attract the media and generate lots of positive publicity for the host venue, thus raising its profile. Equally a competition is attractive for criers because, in return for participating in the event, we are invited to visit a part of the world we might not otherwise see, and enjoy their hospitality. We also have the chance to see other criers in action, swap experiences and enjoy the company of like-minded characters. Comparing notes with fellow town criers is a much-needed therapy. After all there aren't many other men with whom you can safely share the problems you are having with your tights. It's not the kind of conversation that goes down too well at the bar of the local rugby club.

In addition to the hospitality and camaraderie, there is also the possibility of winning a prize or two. Competitions are often fought over two rounds, each round having a different theme. In the first round each crier is usually required to deliver a hometown cry. The competitor will endeavour to promote the virtues of his hometown, and invite hearers to come and visit it for themselves. In this respect the crier is acting as a living holiday brochure.

For the second round a theme will have been set by the host venue. Each crier will have been notified of the theme well in advance, and will have researched and written a cry accordingly. For example at the 2008 Loyal Company of Town Criers British Championship, held in Alnwick, the Alnwick Rum Company was one of the sponsors of the competition, so the theme set for the second round cry was 'Where would you like to drink your Alnwick Rum?' (see page 143). Other themes have included 'Crime and Punishment in Days of Yore' and 'An Historical Newsflash'. In the latter, criers were required to announce an historic event, such as Nelson's victory at the Battle of Trafalgar or the defeat of the Spanish Armada, as if it had just happened. The variety and ingenuity of the cries that are produced is always a delight to spectators and competitors alike, especially as the criers must condense their message within a limit of 125 words.

There's far more to winning a town crier competition than just being loud. In fact excessive loudness could even be marked down if it detracts from audibility. Each cry is judged according to a variety of criteria which may include:

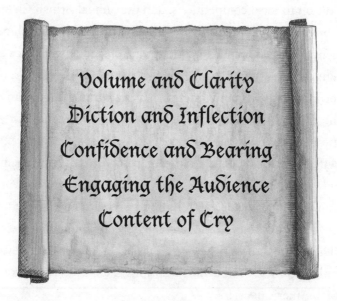

Volume and Clarity
Diction and Inflection
Confidence and Bearing
Engaging the Audience
Content of Cry

At the end of the two rounds, the marks are amalgamated to determine the Champion, and the second and third-place winners. A separate prize is sometimes awarded for the 'Best Content of Cry'. This is occasionally won by a crier who perhaps could not compete with the best criers in terms of delivery, but who has nevertheless excelled in the writing.

The 'Best Ambassador' award is always judged anonymously. The judge of this category discreetly observes the criers' demeanour throughout the day, noting whether they are polite and approachable, and good ambassadors for their town in all circumstances, and not just when they know the spotlight is upon them.

There are also the best dressed categories: 'Best Dressed Crier', 'Best Dressed Escort', and 'Best Dressed Couple'. These categories are judged by separate judges, chosen for their particular expertise in period dress.

All the World's a Stage

Many people I come across assume that town crying is a particularly English tradition. Whilst every civilisation would have needed public proclaimers prior to the development of newspapers and widespread literacy, it is true that England has preserved the tradition more rigorously than any other nation.

In addition to local competitions, and the annual British Championship, an ambitious venue will occasionally stage a World Championship, or World Tournament. Whereas local competitions are staged at weekends and attract a maximum of twenty-five mainly British competitors, a world event is an altogether larger affair, sometimes attracting competitors from across the globe. The event is spread over a whole week, with three or more rounds of competition.

My wife, Julie, and I were privileged to be invited to participate in our first World Championship in 1997. It was held on beautiful Vancouver Island, off the west coast of Canada. We found ourselves in the midst of 63 loud and eccentric criers from four continents, many accompanied by their costumed escorts. The eighteenth-century livery was again very much in evidence, but we were pleased to see colourful exceptions, such as the buckskins worn by some North American criers.

Picture the scene. The competition stage is a bandstand near the shore in Sidney-by-the-Sea. Eagles soar high overhead and whales may be seen surfacing in the Pacific Ocean. As a backdrop, Mount Baker rises up out of the mist, and the beautiful San Juan Islands are spread out before us.

The local airport, at which we recently landed, is very close, and the noise of take-offs and landings could easily disrupt the competition. However, Sidney is so pleased to be hosting this world event that all but the larger aeroplanes are diverted for our convenience. To accommodate the larger aircraft which cannot be diverted to other airports, the Host Crier, Bert Stevens, carries a two-way radio, linked to the control tower, and agrees with Air Traffic Control to make a short break in proceedings while the aeroplanes arrive and depart. What power!

We begin to hear about the legendary Graham Keating, from Australia,

126

who has already won two world championships. As relatively new criers, we hope we will not be out of our depth on the world stage. We are keen to watch and learn, and to catch our first glimpse of Graham Keating in action. He did not disappoint.

After the final cries of the third round, interspersed by an abundance of generous hospitality and sightseeing, we are introduced to another distinctive feature of a World Championship: the Talent Show. Most town criers, being people who have overcome their natural shyness, are able to do a turn; several are professional entertainers.

74. Graham Keating, The Legend

An unforgettable week closes with the Awards Banquet. For newcomers we acquit ourselves reasonably well, and The Legend justifies his reputation: Graham Keating is crowned World Champion yet again. We leave Canada, having learnt a lot, made many new friends, and fallen in love with Vancouver Island.

The competitors have been invited to extend their stay with a trip over the border into the USA. So the next day we climb aboard the ferry which will thread its way through the picturesque San Juan Islands to Sidney's sister-city, Anacortes. We are to travel in livery because when we arrive we will take part in a one-day competition in the town square. It seems like the whole town turns out to greet us as we parade through the streets behind a marching band. So warm and enthusiastic is the welcome we are given that we feel more like a liberating army than town criers.

Mission to the Penal Colonies

The following year, 1998, we are invited to take part in the State of Victoria Championship, in Melbourne, Australia. The competition is a weekend event, but the Australian criers kindly offer hospitality to the English competitors, so that we are able to extend our stay over a period of three weeks. This is indeed a huge perk for criers. We are able to travel to countries we wouldn't otherwise see, and to enjoy fabulous hospitality while we are there. As criers in their communities, our hosts are able to give us access to experiences which wouldn't be available to us as ordinary tourists. In Melbourne, for example, radio and TV seek us out for interviews and we are given a formal reception by the British Consul. We are the Mayor's guests of honour at the Colac Ferret Cup, a great-fun spoof event which is run in imitation of the Melbourne Cup, but instead of horses galloping, Colac has ferrets racing through plastic tubes.

In Sale we stay with the Sale Crier Darren McCubbin and his delightful wife, Gill. Meanwhile, Julie is suffering from an ear infection that she probably picked up on the flight from Manchester. Eventually she goes to see a doctor in Sale. She is surprised to see a doctor wearing shorts who greets

75. Julie Mitchell at the Colac Ferret Cup

her with 'G'day!' She explains, 'I am visiting here from England. I'm staying with your town crier and I've got ear-ache.' The Aussie doctor replies, 'Well, what do you expect?'

I should add that, notwithstanding the good-humoured informality, the doctor is thoroughly professional and treats the ear-ache effectively. Furthermore Darren and Gill are perfect hosts, and become our good friends.

Bringing It All Back Home

Sidney-by-the-Sea was evidently so delighted to have been invaded by such colourful characters that the town hosts a second World Championship in 1999. This time we return home with trophies. Graham Keating is World Champion yet again, but I beat him – and everyone else – in the third-and-final round, and am placed third overall. Julie is placed sixth, making her the world's highest-placed female crier.

The spectacular natural beauty of Vancouver Island creates an unforgettable setting for a World Championship. We return to Chester inspired to bring it all back home, and host a World Tournament in the heart of our own historic city, where proclamations have been made at the High Cross since the Middle Ages.

Chester caught the vision and thus far we have hosted three world tournaments here, in 2001, 2004 and 2010. Every host crier naturally seeks to introduce a new dimension to his event, as well as maintaining the high standards of previous events. Our goal in 2004 was to attract competitors from countries that had not previously been represented. We knew that historically there was a strong tradition of town crying in France, but no one in the crier fraternity was aware of any contemporary French criers; the tradition seemed to have died out there. As it happened, in the summer of 2003 we took a family holiday in the Lot region of France. We visited the small town of Cajarc and asked at the local Tourist Information Office if any town in the region had a town crier, or *crieur public*. To our astonishment they said, 'Yes, we have one here. He lives just down the street and round the corner.' We could hardly believe it.

Armed with his address, five minutes later we were knocking on his door.

When Charles Laparra answered, we explained that we were town criers from England. Now it was his turn to be astonished. He invited us in and explained that up to this moment he thought he was the only town crier left in the world. We told him that not only did he have a huge family of brothers and sisters spread across the globe, but also forty of them would be gathering together in Chester the following summer. 'Why don't you come and be part of it?' we asked. He didn't take much persuading.

76. Charles Laparra, Crieur Public of Cajarc, France

Charles not only added another nation to our World Tournament, but also another attention-gaining device because he uses a drum rather than a handbell (see photo adjacent). Despite having not competed before, and having to write his cries in English, Charles Laparra performed superbly, and was placed tenth. His drumming at the head of parades also brought a much-appreciated, added dimension.

We very much wanted the African continent to be represented. Eventually we made contact with Wilson Sulukazana, the Whale Crier of Hermanus, on the southernmost tip of South Africa. Apparently it is Wilson's role to notify the tourists whenever whales can be seen off the coast of Hermanus, and to this end he uses a kelp horn, another distinctive attention-gaining device. I vividly recall a telephone conversation to Hermanus, trying to persuade Wilson to make the journey to Chester. 'If you can just get your airfare to Manchester, Wilson, we will take care of you while you are in England. We will put you in a hotel in Chester with a west-facing room, and whenever you look out of your bedroom window I guarantee that you will see W(h)ales.'

77. Wilson Salukazana,
the Whale Crier of Hermanus,
at the Chester World Town
Crier Tournament

78. Lord Mayor of Chester, Councillor Reggie Jones, signs the invitations to the Lord Mayor of Chester's Invitational World Town Crier Tournament 2001

Better Than Brochures

Having gathered together forty of the world's most eccentric and extrovert characters, all dressed in colourful period liveries, and most accompanied by their costumed escorts, we obviously had a great number of options to attract the print and broadcast media.

The criers themselves tend to be very media-aware and generate their own media angles. For example, Martin Wood, the Town Crier of Shrewsbury, is seven feet two inches tall, which makes him the world's tallest town crier. His handbell is the size of an average bucket.

Prior to the World Tournament he ran a competition in his local paper for readers to write one of his competition cries. He also persuaded the local railway network to run a special service between Shrewsbury and Chester on competition days, re-naming the service *The Martin Wood Special*, and offering two-for-the-price-of-one fares.

Within minutes of arriving at his Chester hotel, the media descended on him to do a story on how the hotel was extending his bed to accommodate his size. And all this publicity for just one crier before the competition even started. All the criers have their own unique claims to fame, and as you can imagine, none are camera-shy.

The financial outlay necessary for a venue to stage such a colourful, loud and media-friendly spectacle is surprisingly modest. The main requirement is simply to accommodate and feed the participants during their stay. Additional costs include transport, mementoes and prizes. It will be immediately appreciated that this is a relatively inexpensive option for any venue to stage a world event. We don't require special stadia to be constructed, roads to be closed or security and policing to be paid for. A world town crier tournament does no damage to the environment (except possibly the generation of hot air) and requires no clean-up operation afterwards. In short it is highly cost-effective.

The World Tournament held in Chester in June 2001 illustrates the point. The response from the media far exceeded our highest expectations. The broadcast media alone included: *Good Morning TV*, Granada TV, *The Big Breakfast*, Welsh National TV, Welsh Regional TV, BBC National & Regional

TV, *BBC News 24*, HTV, S4C, BBC Wales, BBC World Service (a four-minute broadcast to *every* English-speaking recipient of the World Service), and even Russian TV.

The Lord Mayor, Councillor Graham Proctor, aptly summed up the benefits to Chester of this high profile event. Addressing fellow councillors, sponsors, judges and the world's criers at the Awards Banquet he enthused: 'You have brought the sight of our beautiful City to the world's media. It's been *incredible* how much coverage you have given us and we are very, very grateful for it. Absolutely superb! You collectively have done more for this City than brochures and leaflets could ever do.'

The event as a whole illustrated the feel-good, win-win characteristic so often associated with town criers. The criers enjoyed a fabulous week of generous hospitality in this beautiful city; residents and visitors were treated to the spectacle of colourful and noisy re-enactment; and the city itself harvested massive positive publicity for a relatively modest outlay.

79. The Town Criers and escorts who took part in the Lord Mayor's Invitational World Town Crier Tournament 2001

80. Richard Riddell
(Anacortes, Washington, USA)

81. John Neitz
(Minneapolis, Minnesota, USA)

82. Daniel Richer dit La Flêche
(Ottawa/Gatineau, Canada)

83. Chris Whyman
(Kingston, Ontario, Canada)

12

CONTEMPORARY CRIES

Before a proclamation can be made, it must first be written, and it must be written concisely. This is true for two reasons. Firstly, people walking across the town square, or just passing by where the crier has taken his stand, will more readily absorb a sound bite than a lengthy discourse. And secondly, if the crier is to remain effective throughout a stint spanning several hours, he must protect his voice by not crying at full power for too long on each occasion.

Historically, if a proclamation was of great importance, the crier would be given the exact wording to proclaim by the relevant authority, usually the Sheriff or the City Assembly. Several such cries have been reproduced in this book already. However, for local, everyday announcements, the crier would be given latitude to frame his own cries, and each crier would in time develop his own distinctive style. For example, writing cries in rhyme has a definite historical precedent, and one that several modern-day criers emulate.

Cries made in competitions have other constraints, both in terms of word limits and opening and closing salutations. This is to ensure that competitors are judged against a common yardstick.

As this is a book all about crying, I should, of course, include some contemporary cries. In one respect I hesitate to do so. My hesitation is that a cry, like a song, may begin as words on a page, but it is written to be heard rather than read. A song will be heard as lyrics, melody, harmonies, voice and music. Similarly the cry as written will have added to it the crier's intonation, pauses, emphases, inflection, gestures and other verbal and non-verbal devices which bring the cry to life. So please bear in mind that these specimen cries are like the lyrics on a page; they are not the full delivery.

I would like you to get the full impact of the cries that follow, so if you have bought the deluxe version of this book, you should now turn up the volume to maximum. You will find the slider control built into the spine of the book. If you opted for the cheaper version, just use your imagination.

84.

The theme for the first round in most competitions is a hometown cry in which the crier extols the virtues of his hometown and invites the listeners to come and see it for themselves. In this respect the crier acts as a travelling visitor guide and brochure, and a very effective one too when you consider that the cry may be witnessed and recorded by the media as well as noted by those immediately present. Inventive criers can always find something attractive to say about their hometowns . . .

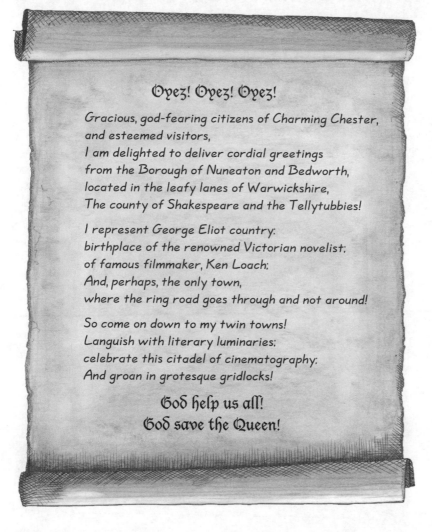

Oyez! Oyez! Oyez!

Gracious, god-fearing citizens of Charming Chester,
and esteemed visitors,
I am delighted to deliver cordial greetings
from the Borough of Nuneaton and Bedworth,
located in the leafy lanes of Warwickshire,
The county of Shakespeare and the Tellytubbies!

I represent George Eliot country:
birthplace of the renowned Victorian novelist:
of famous filmmaker, Ken Loach;
And, perhaps, the only town,
where the ring road goes through and not around!

So come on down to my twin towns!
Languish with literary luminaries;
celebrate this citadel of cinematography;
And groan in grotesque gridlocks!

God help us all!
God save the Queen!

Paul Gough is, by his own admission, 'the most handsome town crier in the known universe'. In a career that now spans over 20 years he has enjoyed great success in competitions, winning over 150 championships, including the Lord Mayor of Chester's Invitational in the year 2000. This is the hometown cry that he proclaimed on that occasion with his customary style and panache.

John Stevens, Town Crier of Alnwick, takes a tongue-in-cheek approach to the task of making a hometown cry, with great effect. He delivers his cry in appropriate Northumbrian dialect, hence 'owerrun' (overrun), 'wor' (our), 'nowt' (nothing), 'toon' (town), and 'haway' (come on!).

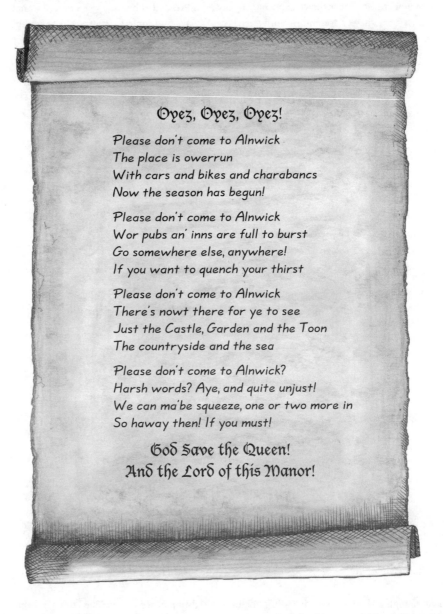

Oyez, Oyez, Oyez!

Please don't come to Alnwick
The place is owerrun
With cars and bikes and charabancs
Now the season has begun!

Please don't come to Alnwick
Wor pubs an' inns are full to burst
Go somewhere else, anywhere!
If you want to quench your thirst

Please don't come to Alnwick
There's nowt there for ye to see
Just the Castle, Garden and the Toon
The countryside and the sea

Please don't come to Alnwick?
Harsh words? Aye, and quite unjust!
We can ma'be squeeze, one or two more in
So haway then! If you must!

God Save the Queen!
And the Lord of this Manor!

John Stevens' full title is 'Bellman to the Common Council of the Burgess of Alnwick' but he is known locally as the 'Common Bellman'. His livery is based on the Duke of Northumberland's Coachman in the Duke's colours of blue and gold. 'The coat is quite long and I am quite short so I am visually likened to a cross between a Dalek and a Toby Jug.'

Town criers rigorously maintain a tradition of loyalty to the ruling monarch, almost invariably concluding every cry with an expression of that loyalty in the words 'God Save the Queen!' In the year of the Queen's Golden Jubilee many criers chose to reaffirm that loyalty. Here is Michael Wood's Jubilee Cry.

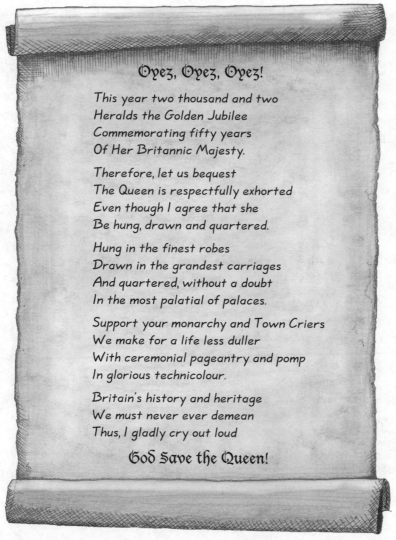

Oyez, Oyez, Oyez!

This year two thousand and two
Heralds the Golden Jubilee
Commemorating fifty years
Of Her Britannic Majesty.

Therefore, let us bequest
The Queen is respectfully exhorted
Even though I agree that she
Be hung, drawn and quartered.

Hung in the finest robes
Drawn in the grandest carriages
And quartered, without a doubt
In the most palatial of palaces.

Support your monarchy and Town Criers
We make for a life less duller
With ceremonial pageantry and pomp
In glorious technicolour.

Britain's history and heritage
We must never ever demean
Thus, I gladly cry out loud

God Save the Queen!

Michael Wood has been the Town Crier for the East Riding of Yorkshire since 1997. He has enjoyed great success in town crier competitions, which includes winning the Lord Mayor of Chester's Invitational World Town Crier Tournament in 2001, the Ancient and Honourable Guild of Town Criers World Championship in 2003 in Newquay, Cornwall, and the 2nd Millennium World Championship in 2000 in Ghent, Belgium. The latter title he holds for a thousand years until the year 3,000, for which he is arranging to defend by asking his council to send his ashes and a tape recording of his voice to the host venue.

In the 2001 World Tournament in Chester the competitors were required to write and proclaim a 'cry from history', that is to say a proclamation from an historical date but announced as if the event in question had just happened. This is David McKee's historical cry.

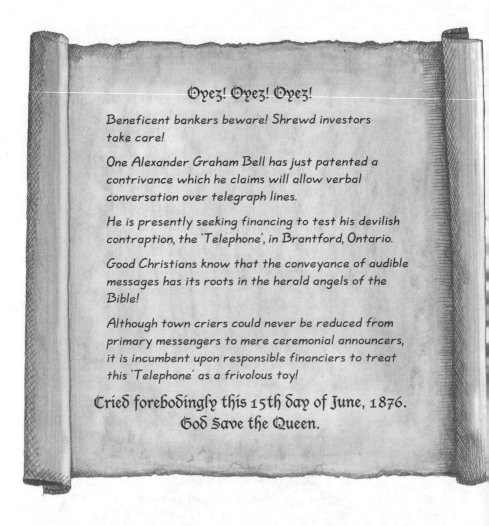

Oyez! Oyez! Oyez!

Beneficent bankers beware! Shrewd investors take care!

One Alexander Graham Bell has just patented a contrivance which he claims will allow verbal conversation over telegraph lines.

He is presently seeking financing to test his devilish contraption, the 'Telephone', in Brantford, Ontario.

Good Christians know that the conveyance of audible messages has its roots in the herald angels of the Bible!

Although town criers could never be reduced from primary messengers to mere ceremonial announcers, it is incumbent upon responsible financiers to treat this 'Telephone' as a frivolous toy!

Cried forebodingly this 15th day of June, 1876. God Save the Queen.

Since May 25, 1992, David McKee has been town crier for the historic City of Brantford, Canada, where Alexander Graham Bell invented the telephone in 1874.

David was placed second and third, respectively, at the 2001 and 2004 Lord Mayor of Chester's Tournaments, second place in the 2001 World Championships and five times winner of the Ontario Guild of Town Criers Provincial Championships.

In competitions the tradition is that the Host Crier doesn't take part in his or her own competition but instead acts as host and compere. This is a sensible precaution against accusations of bias because one of the Host Crier's duties is to appoint the judges, usually from the locality. If the Host Crier were to go on to win the competition, spurred on by local supporters, and judged by local judges, the other competitors might have good reason to feel aggrieved. The Host Crier is still required to cry though, making a benchmark cry, against which all other competitors are judged. This was the benchmark cry made by Julie Mitchell for the Lord Mayor of Chester's Invitational World Town Criers Tournament 2004.

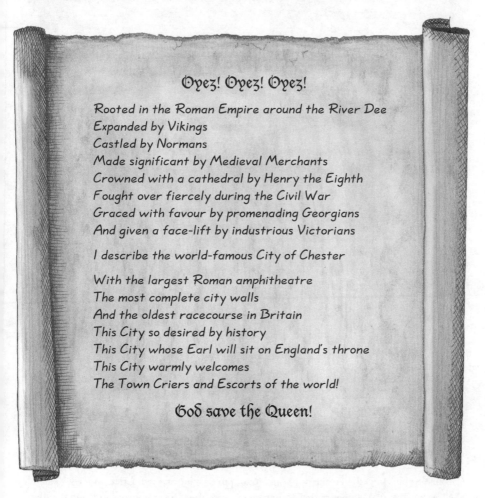

Oyez! Oyez! Oyez!

Rooted in the Roman Empire around the River Dee
Expanded by Vikings
Castled by Normans
Made significant by Medieval Merchants
Crowned with a cathedral by Henry the Eighth
Fought over fiercely during the Civil War
Graced with favour by promenading Georgians
And given a face-lift by industrious Victorians

I describe the world-famous City of Chester

With the largest Roman amphitheatre
The most complete city walls
And the oldest racecourse in Britain
This City so desired by history
This City whose Earl will sit on England's throne
This City warmly welcomes
The Town Criers and Escorts of the world!

God save the Queen!

As well as being jointly Town Crier of Chester along with her husband David, Julie Mitchell is also Chester's Beadle, and believed to be the world's only lady beadle. Historically one of the Beadle's responsibilities was to protect the mayor during his public appearances.

In addition to her Chester appointments, Julie is also Town Crier of Knutsford, and an historical livery maker. In 2009 she won the Best Dressed Town Crier award at the LCTC British Championship in a livery that she designed and made herself.

In 2004 Chester hosted the Warburton's Ladies World Town Crier Tournament. This was the first, and so far only, ladies-only competition at world level. In the second round the competitor's were given the provocative theme, 'A Woman's Place'. Here is the cry proclaimed that day by Caroline Robinson, Town Crier of Palmerston North, New Zealand.

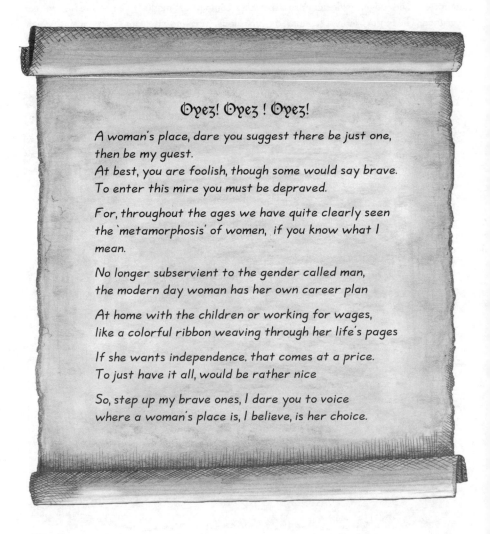

Oyez! Oyez! Oyez!

A woman's place, dare you suggest there be just one,
then be my guest.
At best, you are foolish, though some would say brave.
To enter this mire you must be depraved.

For, throughout the ages we have quite clearly seen
the 'metamorphosis' of women, if you know what I
mean.

No longer subservient to the gender called man,
the modern day woman has her own career plan

At home with the children or working for wages,
like a colorful ribbon weaving through her life's pages

If she wants independence. that comes at a price.
To just have it all, would be rather nice

So, step up my brave ones, I dare you to voice
where a woman's place is, I believe, is her choice.

Caroline Robinson is the President of the Honourable Guild of Town Criers in New Zealand. She was the eventual winner of the Warburton's Ladies Town Crier Tournament, and therefore Women's World Champion.

One of the sponsors of the Loyal Company of Town Criers British Championship 2008, held in Alnwick, was the Alnwick Rum Company. For the second-round cry competitors were required to write a cry on the theme, 'Where and in what circumstances would you like to drink your Alnwick Rum?' This cry evidently went down well with the judges who, unusually, gave the crier maximum marks in both the 'Content of Cry' and 'Engaging the Audience' categories. Crying in rhyme has historic precedent. The structure changes in the last verse because the ending, 'God Save the Queen!', was obligatory in the rules.

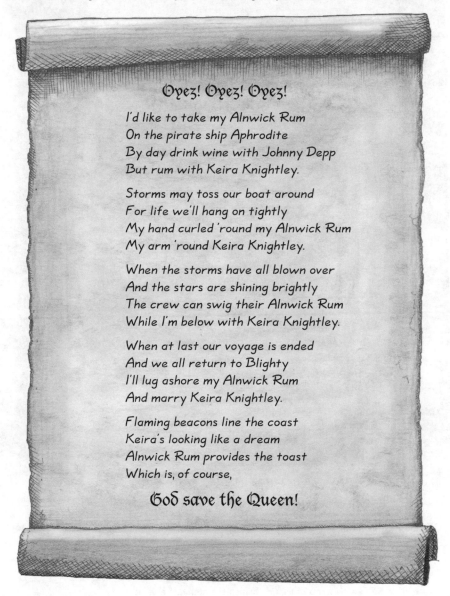

Oyez! Oyez! Oyez!

I'd like to take my Alnwick Rum
On the pirate ship Aphrodite
By day drink wine with Johnny Depp
But rum with Keira Knightley.

Storms may toss our boat around
For life we'll hang on tightly
My hand curled 'round my Alnwick Rum
My arm 'round Keira Knightley.

When the storms have all blown over
And the stars are shining brightly
The crew can swig their Alnwick Rum
While I'm below with Keira Knightley.

When at last our voyage is ended
And we all return to Blighty
I'll lug ashore my Alnwick Rum
And marry Keira Knightley.

Flaming beacons line the coast
Keira's looking like a dream
Alnwick Rum provides the toast
Which is, of course,

God save the Queen!

David Mitchell, Town Crier of Chester

FOR CRYING OUT LOUD!

Graham Keating, Town Crier of Sydney, is a living legend amongst town criers, having been World Champion on no less than five occasions, as well as Australian National Champion an amazing fifteen times. I am pleased to be able to reproduce one of his cries below. This will give some idea of his humour but cannot, unfortunately, convey the effortless projection and clarity of his voice, or his distinctive style and bearing.

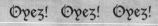

Oyez! Oyez! Oyez!

When the tall ships came to the Great South Land, they heard the cry of "Mooktura!" which is Aboriginal for "Go away!"

We were then settled by two kinds - those who were convicted and those who ought to have been.

Then came the Scots - who pray on their knees and their neighbours.

The Welsh - who keep the Sabbath and anything else they can lay their hands on.

And the Irish - who don't know what they want, but are willing to fight for it anyway.

I am Irish!

My name means "swamp-dweller".

My great, great, grandfather was a convict.

His crime was - he stood outside a laundry in Dublin.

The sign read — "Drop your trousers here, for the best results."

And he did!

God Save the Queen!

Graham Keating has won the World Town Crier Championship on no fewer than five occasions:
- 1991 - Shanklin, Isle of Wight, U.K.
- 1993 - Markham, Ontario, Canada.
- 1997 - Sidney, Vancouver Island, British Columbia, Canada.
- 1999 - Sidney, Vancouver Island, British Columbia, Canada.
- 2001 - Anacortes, Washington State, U.S.A.

13

ASK ME ANOTHER!

From the very first moment that you put on the outfit, or 'livery' as it is more correctly called, and hit the streets as a town crier, you notice that people's reactions to you change dramatically. The appearance of a town crier seems to say to people that you are approachable, that you are happy to be photographed with them, and that you will probably know the answer to any question they may ask.

I anticipated that, as town crier to such an historic city, the questions would largely be about Chester's history. The reality is quite different. Questions about history are rare. Tourists' needs are more practical and immediate: 'Where can I find a bank?', 'Where are the toilets?', 'Where do you recommend for lunch?' and 'Where is Lakeland Plastics?' are the recurring questions that account for 95 per cent of all enquiries.

Children, of course, ask, 'Are you a pirate?' or, more memorably, 'Were you alive once?' But the surprising bonus is the sudden and entertaining question that catches you unawares. 'What time does Wales open for the day?', 'If I call my Aunt Bertha in Adelaide will she be home now?', or 'Can you show me how to go to the toilet?' are all questions guaranteed to brighten your day.

Visitors from the United States of America are a particularly rich source of entertaining enquiries. In fact when they first see someone like me, dressed in tricorne hat, greatcoat, breeches and buckled shoes, they often seem unsure whether I am a re-enactor, or someone who has lived for a particularly long time. It is, of course, well known that our colonial cousins are fascinated by our history, but sometimes their understanding lags behind their enthusiasm.

This comes out in their questions. For example, an American visitor asked, 'Say, you look like the kinda guy who would know pretty much everything around here – can you tell my wife and I where we can get a video of the Great Fire of London?' Now as a town crier I am paid to be polite to the tourists so I must answer helpfully, but deep down I would love to reply, 'Oh, you must mean the one directed by Samuel Pepys.'

Complete Circuit

One of our claims to fame in Chester is having the most continuous city walls in the country. So one day, as I was on those walls, I was approached by an American tourist couple. Our conversation went like this:

Tourist Lady: I understand that you can walk all the way around the city on top of the walls here in Chester. Is that right?

Town Crier: That's right, Madam.

Tourist Lady: So am I right in thinking that you can get on the walls at one point, go all the way around the City, and get off the walls again at the same point you got on at?

Town Crier: That's right, Madam.

Tourist Lady: So tell me, how far would it be to do that complete circuit?

Town Crier: Exactly two miles, Madam.

Tourist Lady: (turning to her husband) You know, Elmer, we should do that while we're here, so that we can tell the folks back home we've been all the way around the City of Chester on top of the walls.

Tourist Lady: (turning back to the town crier) Two miles you say? So tell me, which would be the shortest direction to go in?

Seeing the Light

One has to be prepared for the fact that not all questions will be polite. One American lady was clearly irritated when she asked,

'Say, why do your street lights keep making that strange beeping sound?'

'I don't know what you mean, Madam. Can you show me?'

She indicated the lights at a pelican crossing.

'So what's going on here?'

'Well, it's basically the same as you have in the States, Madam. It's red for stop and green for go.'

She was clearly not satisfied: 'Yeah, yeah, I know *that*. I know that! But what I'm asking you, young man, is why do we get that strange *beeping* sound every time the lights change colour?'

'Well Madam, that's an auditory confirmation for blind people who wouldn't otherwise see the change of colour.'

She was outraged: 'My God! That is awful! That is really terrible! That's the worst thing I've heard since I've been over here! In the States we don't allow blind people to drive!'

Double Take

I want to tell you about another encounter I had with an American tourist, but first I need to introduce you to my best friend for over thirty years: John Spencer. He and I share a fondness for bookshops and we often spend Saturday mornings wandering from bookshop to bookshop, interspersed by visits to coffee shops.

We continued this tradition when I became Chester's town crier, but with one difference: I would now be in my town crier outfit, ready to do the midday proclamation. However, as far as I was concerned, I first had a couple of hours to indulge in books and coffee and conversation. I wouldn't actually take up my town crier duties until nearly midday.

Now although John and I are friends, we are often taken to be brothers because we apparently look alike (an observation more flattering for him than for me). On this particular occasion we went into a coffee shop with a large window facing onto one of the main streets. When we went up to the counter to order our coffees, the waitress said to us, 'Excuse me for asking, but are you twins?'

This amused us greatly, and we were still laughing about it when a tourist walked past the cafe window, saw my outfit and stopped dead in her tracks. After a brief hesitation she walked into the cafe and up our table.

'Excuse me, sir,' she said to me, 'Would you mind stepping out onto the sidewalk so that I could take your picture?'

I replied, 'Well I'm just having a coffee break now, but if you'd care to come to the High Cross at noon for the midday proclamation you can get as many pictures as you want.'

She answered, 'Oh yeah, I know that. I read about you in the brochure. But you see we have to get back on our bus at half-past eleven to head for our next destination. So please, sir, would you mind stepping out onto the sidewalk?'

She was so polite and enthusiastic, and I didn't want to disappoint her. So I said that if she wouldn't mind waiting just a couple of minutes for us to finish our coffees, I'd be delighted to join her 'on the sidewalk'.

I know from experience that tourists usually prefer to be in the photograph with the crier so, just to amuse John, and with the recent twins question in mind, I said to her, 'Why don't you give the camera to my twin brother so that we can both be on the picture together?'

She enthusiastically agreed to this proposal and gave her camera to John. But then, to my surprise, John took up the story: 'Yes, *our mother*, from the very first moment she realised that she was going to have twins, resolved there and then that she would never dress us the same. Today it's his turn to wear the outfit, but if you had come to Chester yesterday, or tomorrow, it would have been my turn.'

Needless to say, I didn't have any trouble smiling for the photograph. But this bizarre conversation wasn't over. She then turned to me and said, 'Thank you. Now would you mind taking the camera and getting a picture of me with your twin brother?'

Neither of us had the presence of mind to ask where in the States she came from but, wherever it was, we like to imagine her showing the photographs to family and friends, explaining: 'Well it all depends which day you visit Chester. It could be him wearing the outfit, or it could be his twin brother.'

85. The author (right) with his 'twin brother', John.

Denver, Colorado

Prior to becoming a town crier, I was a primary school teacher for sixteen years. In fact the move into town crying was a logical career progression: I went from shouting at children to shouting at grown ups.

Now in all those sixteen years no one ever said to me, 'Oh, a school teacher. How fascinating! Tell me, how did you get into that?'

But 'How did you get into it?' is the most frequently-asked question I am asked as a town crier. It's a long story, and telling it repeatedly can sometimes become tedious.

On one particular Saturday morning I was asked that question three times as I chatted to tourists prior to the midday proclamation. When it was over, as usually happens, several tourists stayed behind for photographs.

An American couple were especially enthusiastic and we chatted happily as I posed first with my arm around the lady's shoulders while the husband took a photograph, and then shook his hand while she pressed the shutter. All was going perfectly until he said, 'So tell me, how did you come to get this job in the first place?'

I thought, 'Oh no! I can't face telling that same story yet again. Perhaps they would be happy with a brief quip.' So I answered:

'Well actually it was my parole officer's idea. He said that they were prepared to let me out six months early if I was willing to take the job.'

They didn't laugh, as I had expected they would, but nodded sympathetically and understandingly. Then, to my surprise, the lady moved very close to me, and looked first over one shoulder, then over the other, to make sure no one was close enough to overhear what she was going to say next. She dropped her voice to a subdued whisper before confiding:

'Yeah, we know what you mean. It was like that with our son back in Denver, only for what he did, they had him picking up litter from the streets.'

I realised, to my amazement that they had taken me seriously. They clearly thought that, as a complete stranger, I had confided in them an embarrassing incident from my own life, and they had reciprocated by sharing a family secret from their side. There was no going back once I realised that they'd taken me seriously. I couldn't say, 'Well, I was only joking', because by then they were already committed. They would feel so exposed. I couldn't think of anything to do or say, except that it was now my turn to nod sympathetically and understandingly. But even as I did so, I couldn't help but think that within a week, or a fortnight at most, they would be back in the States, they would have had their photographs processed, and they would be showing them to all their friends: 'This is us in the quaint little old city of Chester. And this is us with the town crier.' But when they came to show the photographs to their son – well you know what it's like as a parent, you don't miss an opportunity to drive home a moral – they'd be sure to say, 'You just be grateful, son, that we live in Denver, Colorado, because if we'd lived in Chester, England, for what you did they'd have had you walking the streets in a wig and tights!'

150

Forbidden Fruit

I am often asked to give talks to various groups and organisations. It is a great privilege, and huge pleasure, to travel all over the country speaking about this unusual lifestyle. Speaking in old people's homes, however, presents particular challenges. Some of your audience will be asleep before you start and others will drop off before you finish. But more disconcerting are those who wake up half way through and cry out, 'Where am I?'

I had finished one such presentation and was afterwards asked by the matron if she could take pictures of me in my outfit with some of the residents. I agreed, of course, and was asked to pose with Dorah. Now Dorah was just a few days short of her hundredth birthday, frail and stooped. I thought I'd do exactly as I do with the tourists in Chester: pose with my arm around her shoulder. But she wasn't having any of it. She immediately stiffened and backed away: 'Not so close young man, not so close! Forbidden fruit, remember!'

Bins Day

I have perhaps given the impression that the bizarre questions are always asked by American tourists. Well they do come up with some peaches, but one of the most astonishing questions was asked by a Chester resident. My predecessor as Chester's town crier, David Maguire, was giving a talk about his job to a retirement group in Chester. He began by briefly mentioning how he was appointed to the post by Chester City Council (as indeed I am). There then followed a forty-five minute account of the variety of things a town crier is called upon to do. Afterwards he was asked to take questions.

A man at the back immediately shot up his hand. I can only assume that his mention of Chester City Council had led him to assume that a town crier's influence with that organisation was more far-reaching than it really is.

'Yes Sir, what's your question?' David asked.

'Can you tell me, Mr. Maguire, why our bins weren't emptied last Tuesday?'

Let me be frank with you, dear reader. If you are having problems with your refuse collection, in Chester or elsewhere, I'm sorry but I really cannot help you. On the other hand, if you have someone who needs a jolly good shouting at, I could be just your man.

86. Town Crier and Apprentice on their way to make the midday proclamation at the High Cross

14

ABDOMINAL RESONATORS

The stereotype of a town crier is of a very large, round-bellied man with a booming voice. And it's true that some criers put themselves forward for the job because they are naturally loud. When I was first appointed, I was anything but naturally loud. Furthermore I knew that if I didn't learn to project my voice properly, I would probably develop nodules on my larynx and have a very short career. I needed technique and I needed it fast. But where could I go to learn the technique?

Now if I have a problem to solve, I like, if at all possible, to read about it. The search for a book on how to shout without damaging your voice wasn't easy but I eventually discovered *Voice and the Stage* by Daphne Jacobs, and found myself in a whole new world – the world of the professional voice user.

The book was initially more mystifying than enlightening. On nearly every page I encountered the word 'diaphragm' and the importance of using it correctly to project the voice. By the time I had finished the book I could spell 'diaphragm', which, I hope you will agree, is no small accomplishment. But I had no idea how to use it. In fact I didn't even know what it *was*. I had a vague concept that it was the inside bit of my belly button, the bit you can't see. Furthermore, very early on in the book the author stated that 'it is very difficult to learn to do voice exercises from reading a book'. I couldn't help but wonder, 'So why did you write it?'

Having read the book, yet being unable to implement the advice, I wrote to the author, care of the publishers, to ask if she would give me lessons.

At this point I should explain that I come from a South Derbyshire mining village where we say 'kupp' and 'buss'. If we see a fair maiden we greet her with 'Ay up, me duck!' Our idea of *haute cuisine* is black puddin' and bread and drippin'. Our concept of culture, or 'kultcha' as we call it, is brass bands, boxin' and pidgin-racin'. We don't come across ladies who paint their finger nails red and talk of 'slipping on the parth and having my leg encased in a plarster carst'. However I was soon to discover that the world of professional voice training is dominated by the 'plarster carst' brigade.

It obviously took some time for my letter to be forwarded to the author, so when the telephone rang several weeks later I was unprepared.

'Hello. This is Daphne Jacobs here. I have received your letter but I'm afraid I am far too busy to take on a new pupil. But I do have a colleague, Janice Chivers, at the Voice Department of the Royal Shakespeare Company in Stratford upon Avon. And she's very good. So if you would like me to, I can pass on your request to her.'

I would have preferred perhaps to have found tuition more locally, and would not normally have aspired as high as the Royal Shakespeare Company for my fledgling experience of voice work, but with no other options on the horizon I gratefully accepted her kind offer.

Several more weeks passed by, and again I was at home, thinking about something entirely different, when the telephone rang. Now people will often introduce themselves at the beginning of the call, but if you don't already know the person, the name isn't helpful until you get the context. In retrospect I realise she must have said,

'Hello, this is Janice Chivers from the RSC.'

But I didn't recognise the name and, out of context, I didn't immediately recognise the initials 'RSC'. So I completely got the wrong end of the stick and answered,

'Oh it's all right, I'm with the AA, thank you, and I've already renewed my insurance.'

'No, no, you don't understand. *The RSC* – the Royal Shakespeare Company – in Stratford upon Avon. I've had your letter passed on to me by Daphne Jacobs and I would be delighted to work with you, if you could make your way to the Voice Department here at the RSC in Stratford.'

She went on to explain that by 'delighted' she meant at £60 an hour. We agreed a date and time. She instructed me to ask for her at the stage door when I arrived, and she would come down to meet me and escort me to the Voice Department. Before we ended the conversation, I asked her if she worked with anyone famous. She didn't seem to like that question, but replied,

'Well, I am currently working with someone you may have heard of: John Nettles.'

'Wow!' I thought, 'Bergerac!'

It was a mistake to have asked that question because there was a waiting time of some three or four weeks before my lesson, and in the interim I began to get anxious. I already knew that I didn't understand the business of the diaphragm, but I then started to fantasise about what the Voice Department would be like. I pictured it as a big gymnasium of the voice, with floor-to-ceiling mirrors and imagined that when I arrived for my lesson John Nettles would be working with his teacher in one corner, Kenneth Branagh in another, Helena Bonham-Carter in a third, and me in the other corner, completely out of my depth.

So you can appreciate that I was in a state of anxiety and insecurity when I arrived at the theatre for my first lesson. I asked for Janice Chivers at the stage door, and the man there phoned through to the Voice Department. Now I had only spoken to this lady on the phone so I had no idea what she looked like, or what age she was. After a few minutes she emerged out of the shadows. I discovered that she was physically striking: young, attractive and shapely. In fact, for the sake of what follows, I need to be more specific than that. How can I put it without being indelicate? She had what we professional voice-users might call 'well-developed upper abdominal resonators'. I only mention that because it becomes relevant.

She led me along a labyrinth of stairways and corridors, and every so often I caught sight of the stage set for the first performance of *The Tempest* that evening. We eventually reached the Voice Department which turned out to be nothing like the elaborate 'gymnasium of the voice' that I had imagined, but a very small room, simply furnished with a couple of chairs, a coffee table and a bookcase.

We sat down and she asked a couple of questions about what I did as a town crier and what I wanted to achieve. But she was very enthusiastic, and wanted to get straight down to work.

'OK, David, let's get started. I'd like you to lie down on your back on the floor.'

The lesson was to last an hour, and that first instruction proved to be the only one I understood.

'Now David, I want you to show me how you fill using your diaphragm.'

My heart sank. I knew that this diaphragm business was sure to come up eventually, and I needed to learn how to use it. But I was hoping to have some success first. To make matters worse, she gave me some further explanation in poetic imagery:

'David, I want you to think of a bright silver bucket. I want you to take that bucket quickly up to the top of the mountain, pause for a moment, and then go racing down into the valley, plunging your bucket into the river and drawing it out again full and overflowing with fresh sparkling water!'

And this was something to do with *breathing!* I had no idea what she was talking about. In the hope of saving face, the only thing I could think to do was to make some random twitching movements in my upper abdomen in the hope that, by sheer chance, some of them would coincide with what she was asking me to do. Evidently none of them did because she said, 'Never mind, David, never mind. Stand up. Let's try a different approach.'

It was then that this young, shapely, attractive lady with the well-developed upper abdominal resonators, came and stood six inches in front of me, turned to face in the opposite direction and said, 'Right, David, I am going to demonstrate filling the abdomen using the diaphragm. I'd like you to put your hands on my intercostals while I fill.' So I did. And that got me breathing.

Foolishly I subsequently made the mistake of telling that story in the presence of my wife, and I haven't been allowed to have any further input from the Royal Shakespeare Company.

(Note: I have changed the names of the people in this story. I wouldn't want 'Janice Chivers' to be suddenly overwhelmed by men seeking voice lessons for the wrong motives.)

15
WILT THOU?

The town crier's role as a walking broadcaster of news has long gone, replaced by newspapers, radio and television. Nowadays no one in their right mind is going to wait until midday to hear the latest news from a man in a wig and tights. But just occasionally I get to announce a genuine news scoop and I'd like to tell you of one such occasion.

One Wednesday evening the telephone rang and a young man introduced himself as Darren Johnson. He told me that 'for the past six months my girlfriend has been giving me earache because she says that I am not romantic enough'.

My first thought was that he had got the wrong number, and that he should really be speaking to Relate or some similar organisation. But he went on to explain, 'I have got a brilliant idea to show my girlfriend just how romantic I can be, and you fit into my plan. On Saturday I am going to bring my girlfriend, Sharon, into Chester for what she will think is just an ordinary Saturday looking around the shops. But I am going to arrange it so that, just before noon, we are passing by the High Cross as you are about to do your midday proclamation. I will then say to Sharon, as if spontaneously, 'Why don't we stop and listen to the town crier?'

'Now I know that, midway through your proclamation, you often invite a volunteer from the audience to come out and read an advertisement from your scroll. Well, on Saturday I am going to volunteer and I want you to choose me because when I get out there, after I have announced the advertisement, I am going to propose to my girlfriend in front of the whole crowd. Then she will see just how romantic I can be!'

Ladies will immediately recognise this as typical male thinking: 'It doesn't matter how unromantic I have been in the past, nor how unromantic I will be in the future, if the gesture is big enough it will make up for all other neglects, past and future!'

I found the prospect immediately exciting. A live proposal in front of a large audience would be real life drama at its best. That Sharon's reaction could not be predicted only added to the excitement. So I said to Darren, 'Look, we really need to meet up and plan this in more detail.' So it was that the following evening we met up in a convenient Chester hostelry, the Coach and Horses in Northgate Street. Darren gave me some background information, and I wrote out a proposal script for him there and then. One thing I have learnt to do as a town crier is to write proclamations in historic-sounding phraseology, so into Darren's outline proposal I inserted a few 'thees' and 'thous' and 'wilt thou plight thy troth unto me', etcetera. I then handed the script to Darren so that he could practise before Saturday. Unbeknown to me, but to his credit, Darren took the script away and learnt it by heart.

When Saturday came I approached the midday proclamation with even more anticipation than usual. Some 200 or so tourists from all around the world had gathered at the High Cross. I scanned the crowd for Darren, and saw him standing halfway back with a girl standing next to him. Having reassured myself that Darren had safely arrived, I didn't look in his direction again because I didn't want any look of recognition to pass between us that might alert Sharon that something was afoot.

When the clock struck noon I went through my usual routine. I welcomed overseas visitors to Chester in their own languages. On that particular day there were tourists from Scotland, Wales, Ireland, France, Germany, Holland, Italy, Spain, Israel, Japan, China, India, Australia, New Zealand, Canada and 'our Colonies in America'. Yes, I am a gifted linguist and can address tourists in each of those languages! Less impressive is that I can only say 'Welcome to Chester!' but they don't know that, and they are invariably delighted with the one sentence which hints that I could easily converse further, if only I had the time.

I announce the significant events that have happened on this date in history, and I ask quiz questions and give out prizes. But my heart isn't really in any of this because I am impatient to get to the part where I declare, 'I do now call upon some person here present to come and read an advertisement from my scroll.'

Well, that's when things start to go wrong. I look out of my corner of my eye at this point, expecting to see Darren eagerly volunteering. But to my alarm Darren is gazing into space as if he isn't even listening. Now my problem is that I have given out the invitation, and any second now some American tourist is going to volunteer because, as you have no doubt noticed, out of a continent of 300 million people there doesn't appear to be a single shy one. And if an American does volunteer, I am going to have to say something like, 'I'm sorry, sir, but I don't like the look of you', because otherwise the whole proposal plan will collapse.

Fortunately no American does volunteer, and I give out the invitation a second time. This time Darren's hand is slowly raised. (Afterwards I tackled Darren about this: 'Why didn't you volunteer at the first time of asking?' 'Well', Darren explained, 'I didn't want to appear too keen in case it gave the game away!' That was a good point, I had to admit, but I wish he had warned me beforehand.)

89. 'Ladies and gentlemen, pray give heed to this noble youth!'

So Darren is now standing beside me, facing the crowd. I hand my scroll to him, and he reads the advertisement for the day, which was about how you can buy souvenir candles from the Chester Candle Shop. He then hands the scroll back to me, and I make as if to continue my proclamation when he (as planned) interrupts me by asking, 'Town Crier! Might I now make an announcement of mine own?'

I feign surprise, pretend to consider his request for a moment before replying, 'By all means! Ladies and gentlemen, I pray you all give heed unto this noble youth!'

90. Wilt thou, Sharon Samantha Edwards . . .

As previously mentioned, Darren had learnt his script by heart and now launches into it with style and gusto. The crowd immediately sense that this is a live proposal, with an uncertain outcome. Being tourists they are, of course, equipped with still and video cameras, and as the drama unfolds the cameras begin to click and whirr. As Darren nears the climax of his proposal he moves closer to Sharon. Immediately the crowd closes in around them, delighted to witness this live drama and capturing it all for posterity. Darren then goes down on one knee and asks, in commendably clear and audible tones, 'Wilt thou, Sharon Samantha Edwards, consent to plight thee thy troth unto me?'

162

Would you like to know what she says? Remember Sharon is the girl who, for the past six months, has been complaining that Darren isn't romantic enough. Darren has planned this very romantic, imaginative and courageous proposal. Everyone is eagerly awaiting her response. I have my bell raised, ready to announce what will hopefully be Sharon's joyful acceptance of Darren's proposal. But Sharon is so overcome that all she can do is cry. And cry she does, continuously, for several minutes. I still have my bell raised in the air, but all the blood is beginning to drain from my arm. Eventually Sharon manages to stop blubbing long enough to say 'Yes!' that she would be delighted to marry Darren. The tourists roar their approval, break out into applause, take more video and photographs and shower the smiling couple with good wishes for their future happiness. The tourists make their farewells and depart.

By 'depart' I don't just mean depart from the Cross, but depart from Chester. Having chatted with many tourists over the years I know that the tour guide will often announce in the hotel at breakfast, 'You can spend the morning looking around Chester's fabulous array of shops, and then at noon go to the High Cross and listen to the town crier's midday proclamation. When he has finished, that will be time for you to board the coach for us to head off to our next destination.' So I thought that the witnesses to Darren's proposal would soon be making their way to Edinburgh, or London or Dublin and that would be the end of it. How wrong I was!

It seems that they were so taken by the whole thing that they were still talking about it when they arrived at their new destinations. As a result I got a phone call from Radio Dublin asking for a telephone interview. Then the story got picked up by several national newspapers. Darren and Sharon both worked at a large financial services organisation in Chester and once the story of Darren's proposal appeared in newspapers, it spread like wildfire around the offices, with this rather delightful consequence: every young girl who read the story turned on her boyfriend and complained, 'Why can't you be as romantic as Darren?!'

16

PRIDE COMETH

You can be asked to do some very strange things as a town crier, but initially this enquiry sounded routine. A lady called me on the telephone and introduced herself as Margaret Parker. She explained that her daughter, Deborah, was soon to be getting married and would I please do an 'olde worlde' proclamation of congratulations as the newly-weds emerge from the church after the ceremony? I looked at my diary, checked that date was free and said, yes, that would be fine. She told me where and at what time the wedding would be and it all seemed straightforward.

'There's just one more thing,' Mrs Parker added. 'My daughter, Deborah, has been mad about horses all of her life and since the age of twelve she has had her own horse called Sooty. The other day she said to me, "Mum, could Sooty be outside the church when Carl and I come out from getting married?" I answered, "Don't be ridiculous Deborah!" But I only said that to put her off the scent because where they are getting married, at Plemstall Church, there's no town, no village even. It's just a pretty fifteenth-century church, next to a farmhouse, surrounded by fields. So, you see, there will be two surprises for Deborah and Carl when they come out of the church . . . you and the horse! If that's all right with you?'

My first reaction was flippant. I said as long as it was me doing the proclamation, not the horse, I didn't mind. But then I remembered the engraving that I have on my study wall at home. The engraving depicts somebody in the eighteenth century, dressed exactly as I do (even down to the tan-topped riding boots) sitting astride a horse making a proclamation to a group of people gathered nearby. Looking at that engraving I had often thought, 'The only way an eighteenth-century town crier could have travelled around was on horseback. There were no other options.' So I said to Mrs Parker, 'Why don't we combine the two surprises? Why don't I sit on the horse to make the announcement?'

'That sounds lovely,' said Mrs Parker, 'but I know you always start a proclamation by ringing your bell, and the horse, not being used to the sound of a bell being rung on its back, might be spooked by it. And if he is spooked, there's no knowing what might happen.'

'Oh,' I replied, disappointed, 'I hadn't thought of that!'

'Well, it might not be an insurmountable problem,' Mrs Parker continued. 'You see, my daughter, Deborah, is a school teacher and she is safely out of the way during the daytime, so, if you are willing, I could arrange for you to come and meet the girl who exercises and grooms the horse during the day. You can try out the horse with the bell and, who knows, after a bit of practice, it might be fine.' This is the kind of bizarre thing that you can find yourself doing as a town crier, having a secret meeting with a horse.

So I go at the appointed time and meet Mrs Parker, who takes me down into the paddock and introduces me to the girl who exercises and grooms the horse. The first thing that I notice about this girl is that she is young and good-looking. She goes into the stable and leads out the horse. The first thing that I notice about the horse is that it's *big*. It is also very good-looking but *very big*. It is only when I am standing next to this massive creature that I realise what a ridiculous thing it is that I am proposing to do: having had no riding experience myself I am going to climb into the saddle of a very big horse to see if I can spook it by ringing a bell on its back. I want to abandon the whole idea right there and then, but the attractive young girl is looking at me expectantly. Male ego obliges me to continue. Even so I resolve to continue cautiously. So I say to the girl, 'I am a bit concerned that if the horse is spooked by the bell, I won't know what to do, because I don't know where any of the pedals are. Would you mind getting on the horse first and seeing how it goes?'

'Certainly,' she agrees. So I prepare to watch her very carefully because in a minute it's going to be my turn and I want to be impressive. I notice how

91. The only way an eighteenth-century crier could have travelled around was on horseback

the girl gathers the reins together in her left hand, jams them together at the front of the saddle, puts her left foot in the stirrup and then, in one smooth and graceful movement, she climbs into the saddle. I think, 'That's going to be me in a minute.'

I hand the bell to her. She holds it at arm's length and gives it a faint tinkle. The horse immediately pricks up its ears. Now I am no horse psychologist, obviously, but to me the horse does not seem to be alarmed. It just seems to be wondering, 'Does this mean food?' When no food is forthcoming, it goes back to chewing the grass. The girl rings the bell a bit louder and a bit closer to its ear. The horse ignores it. Then she rings it at full volume right in its ear. The horse takes not the slightest notice. So I am happy with this and say to the girl, 'Right I am ready to have a go now.'

So she springs gracefully out of the saddle and I get ready to spring in. Remember I have watched her carefully. I jam the reins against the front of the saddle with my left hand as I have seen her do. I put my left foot in the stirrup. My thigh goes into immediate spasm. The springing into the saddle does not happen for me. In the end I have the indignity of this attractive young girl, whom I am trying to impress, having to get her hands under my rump and shove me up and into the saddle.

Then, when I am in the saddle, I realise for the first time that the horse is an optical illusion. From ground level I had already noticed that the horse is very big. When I get into the saddle, the horse is suddenly twice as big as it was when I was on the ground. And, to make matters worse, I start to remember the things that you are taught about horses, how intelligent and sensitive they are. I think to myself, 'This horse knows the girl that exercises it regularly and senses that she knows exactly what she is doing. It already knows that it does not know me and probably senses that I have got no idea what I am doing. So it might behave entirely differently when I ring the bell.'

Again I would have abandoned the project there and then, had it not been for the fact that the attractive young girl is looking at me expectantly. So I have to go ahead. As faintly as possible I tinkle the bell: the horse ignores it. I tinkle it a bit closer and a bit louder: the horse ignores it. And then, emboldened, I ring it at full volume right into his ear: the horse takes not the slightest bit of notice. So all my confidence comes flooding back.

Well, actually that's not quite true. It's not confidence, it's ego. I start to imagine what a sensation I am going to be on the day, in my magnificent outfit on this magnificent horse. I am really getting into it now and I say to the girl, 'Now, as I understand it from Mrs Parker, this is what is going to happen on the day. The horse is going to be delivered by horsebox onto the site, after everyone has gone into the church. Apparently there is a tall hedge conveniently separating the farmhouse from the church. The horsebox will be parked in the farmyard, hidden from view behind the hedge, and the horse will be drawn out of the horsebox at that point. When all the guests come out of the church, we need the horse to walk from behind the hedge and stop just in front of where the guests are gathered. It has been calculated that this will only be about ten to fifteen paces. Then I will need the horse to stand still for three minutes whilst I do the proclamation. After that I just need it to turn and walk away again, back behind the hedge. So please could you talk me through those basic commands: turn, walk and stop. I won't need the horse to trot, canter, gallop, do dressage or anything fancy, just turn, walk and stop.'

'You must be joking! If you want to control a horse to follow those commands, you are going to need a series of lessons.'

'That's not practical. I haven't got the time or the money!'

'Well, there might be an alternative. Am I right in thinking that this is going to be a surprise to the guests?'

'Yes. The only people who know about the plan are the bride's mother, me and now you.'

'Well, think about it. The last thing that the guests will be expecting at a wedding is a horse to come around the corner ridden by a man in eighteenth-century clothing. When that happens, all eyes will be on you!'

"Yes I like the sound of that!"

'So, what could happen is that I come on the day, dressed in my everyday jeans and jumper, so that next to you and the horse I will be unnoticeable. You can have the reins in your hands and *appear* to control the horse, but I can hold this thing we called "the lead rein" and control the horse for you and then there will be no need for any lessons.'

This sounds like the perfect solution. So it is agreed upon, and I am so convinced that I am going to create a marvellous spectacle on the day that I want it recorded for posterity. I call up the *Evening Leader* newspaper and *Cheshire Life* magazine, asking them if they would send their photographers on the day, sworn to secrecy so as not to give the game away. This they agree to do.

92. St Peter's Church, Plemstall

Finally the wedding day arrives. Picture the scene. The guests are inside the church, witnessing the wedding ceremony, totally unaware of the secret plot unfolding outside. The horse arrives by horsebox, which is hidden from view behind the hedge. The horse is led out, and I climb into the saddle. A lookout has been posted to tell us when to break cover. As I am waiting on the horse, I am proudly anticipating how wonderfully impressive I am going to be. There's a certain biblical proverb that becomes relevant at this point: 'Pride cometh before a fall.'

Eventually my lookout comes over to me and says, 'David, now would be the right time. The bride and groom and guests have just come out of the church. They are gathering for the group photograph, so now would be perfect.'

The girl pulls on the lead rein and after two or three steps the horse emerges from behind the hedge and comes into full view. The guests break out into expressions of surprise and delight. The bride smiles beautifully and her eyes fill up with tears of joy. There are many 'oohs' and 'aahs' to be heard.

I lap up all the admiring glances. I make sure that the *Evening Leader* and *Cheshire Life* photographers have the opportunity to take as many photographs as they wish. But eventually I can delay the fateful moment no longer. I remove the bell from the crook of my arm and ring it with a flourish.

The horse takes no notice. Why should it? I am a professional. I have planned and prepared for this situation. Why should anything go wrong? Thorough preparation eliminates unpleasant surprises. We had prepared for this moment so why should anything go wrong? I unfurl the scroll and begin to cry. *'Oyez!!!!'*

The horse goes berserk!

Sooty attempts to gallop off into the distance, but is firmly restrained by the girl holding tightly onto the lead rein. Because it is being restrained by the lead rein it cannot escape the noise, so it expresses its alarm by spinning around furiously. My dignified proclamation becomes a rapidly revolving blur.

I am suddenly terrified by a confusing kaleidoscope of sights and sounds: laughing faces, glimpses of church and gravestones and open fields, a worried-looking bride, open-mouthed press photographers, laughter, rapid heartbeats (mine), high-kicking hooves (Sooty's) and a scroll which cannot be held steady enough to read. Having begun the proclamation I am obliged to continue. But every bellowed sound from me further alarms the horse.

You can only cry effectively at a crowd when you are facing them but after three revolutions I am so dizzy that I can no longer tell where the crowd is. Nor can I read the proclamation to cry it. I fear that at any moment the lead rein will slip from the girl's grasp and the last that will ever be seen of me is as I disappear into the sunset desperately clinging to the saddle. Perhaps the *Evening Leader* and *Cheshire Life* will get a final picture of my retreating rear.

94. Safely back on terra firma, the Chester Town Crier presents a souvenir scroll to Deborah, while Carl and Sooty look on

It takes me ten minutes to get to the end of what should have been a three-minute proclamation. When I finally get to 'God Save the Queen!' and stop shouting, the horse stops spinning. It takes another thirty seconds for the blood to stop spinning in my head before I can focus on the crowd again, whom I have not seen for the past ten minutes. But I remember them as I had last seen them: standing upright, with their smiles of delight and anticipation. The next time I see the crowd, it is as if they have been mown down by a machine gun. None are any longer standing upright. Handkerchiefs are much in evidence. My enduring memory is of the bride's father leaning on the church wall, wiping the tears from his eyes.

My horseback proclamation *was* a sensation, but not in the way I intended. I comfort myself with the thought that the wedding videographer hasn't posted the footage on YouTube. Yet.

17

TIGHTS IN LIGHTS

Being a town crier is wonderfully varied. We get into all kinds of privileged situations. But it does have one inherent danger. Sooner or later you will get the opportunity to become famous. This might seem like a bonus, but actually it can be a poisoned chalice. It will happen when you least expect it, and if you are not very careful, it will go straight to your head and you will make a complete fool of yourself.

For me it happened when I was at home doing something very ordinary. In fact I was ironing my tights at the time, when the telephone rang:

'Hello, this is Stephanie Myhill here. I am the Casting Director for Granada Television. We are currently casting for a film adaptation of *Moll Flanders* which is to be made into four one-hour episodes and shown on television here in Britain, in Canada and the United States of America. The director wants to use a town crier to give some colour to the London street scenes, but he doesn't want to use an actor for this role; he feels it would be far more authentic to use a professional town crier. Now I have auditioned several town criers from all over Britain on the telephone, and so far none of them has proved suitable. If you were to prove suitable, would you be at all interested in this role?'

Interested? She had just used three words which had a magical effect on me: film, television, and most of all, America! The imagination works fast when the ego is engaged, and instantly I found myself mentally rehearsing my Oscar acceptance speech for 'Best Newcomer in a Film'.

However I had yet to win the part. 'Obviously,' I thought, 'if she has already rejected many other candidates, she must have very high standards.' So, I decided to play it cool. 'Tell me more,' I replied. How cool is that?!

'Well,' she explained, 'we have built the London street set, for the scenes in which the town crier would be involved, in a disused sports centre in Warrington, and *if* you were to prove suitable, we would need you to be available to us from seven in the morning until seven in the evening, on Wednesday, Thursday and Friday of next week. You would need to be able to commit for all three days. So before we go any further would you like to check your diary to see if you are free on those dates?'

Hollywood would have been my first choice, but Warrington a close second. I got my diary out, but I was so desperate to be a film star that I just crossed everything out, before answering, with feigned coolness, 'Er . . . yes . . . I think as it happens that I could be free on those dates . . . '

'OK', she continued, 'so now I need to interview you over the telephone.'

I was in the privacy of my own home, but so eager to be a star that I got to my feet and offered up a short but earnest prayer, 'Lord, please let me be a film star!'

The questions she asked were surprisingly mundane. 'How old are you?', 'How tall are you?', 'What period is your costume?' and 'Have you got your own bell?' None of these questions gave me much opportunity to impress, so besides answering the questions that she'd asked, I desperately added anything else that I thought might clinch it for me. I mentioned the Shakespeare play that I'd recently been in and the lessons I'd had at the Voice Department of the Royal Shakespeare Company in Stratford upon Avon. I was even tempted to mention my equestrian experience, but thought better of it.

I didn't think the interview had gone especially well, but she concluded it by saying, 'Well, that's fine Mr Mitchell. You say your costume is late eighteenth century. The film is actually set in the early seventeenth century, but that doesn't matter. I am going to take down your measurements and there will be two costumes ordered and waiting for you when you arrive on set a week on Wednesday.'

'What?' I stammered, 'do you mean I've got the part?'

'Yes,' she confirmed, 'if you can commit to those three days, I am giving you the part of town crier in Granada Television's production of *Moll Flanders*.'

Wow! I should have just been grateful, but my ego was instantly inflated. I thought to myself, 'This lady is a professional casting director. She has auditioned town criers from all over Britain and none of them has proved suitable. And yet, after the briefest of conversations with me, she has given me the part. She must have recognised some star potential in me. And I'd like to know what it is.' So, trying to sound casual, I asked, 'Incidentally, why do you think that I am right for this part?' And then I waited to hear all the flattering things she would say by way of explanation.

'Well, Mr Mitchell, I did audition one gentleman who seemed to be suitable for the part until I asked him how tall he was. He said he was six feet three inches tall. There is nothing particularly exceptional about that these days, but in the early seventeenth century, when standards of health and nutrition were nothing like they are today, that would have been exceptionally tall. I don't want to cast anyone five feet eleven inches or above.

'And then I spoke to another gentleman who was the right height, but when I asked him how old he was, he said he was in his mid-seventies. Now that might be quite normal for town criers of today, but again, in the early seventeenth century, when standards of life expectancy were nothing like they are today, that would have been exceptionally old to be carrying out such a demanding outdoor occupation.

'And then I found someone who was the right height and the right age and right in every other respect, until he mentioned that he'd recently been discharged from hospital, having had one of his legs amputated. We were sensitive to that, but it wasn't quite what we were looking for in the part.

'Now we are getting desperately close to the shooting schedule, Mr Mitchell, and at this late stage what we're really saying is, if you are under six feet tall, less than 60 years of age, and you've still got both your legs, you'll do for us!'

I wish I'd never asked.

95. I was ironing my tights when the telephone rang

I arrived on set early on the Wednesday morning, fired up by all my Oscar-winning ambitions. I discovered that it was only the extras who were required to arrive on set at seven in the morning. And that's what I'd been hired as, an extra. Mind you, I was a *'speaking* extra'. We speaking extras look down on the non-speaking extras. The aim was, apparently, to get all the extras into costume and make-up early, so that the stars could roll in at half past nine and go straight into filming. The stars in this film were, incidentally, Alex Kingston, Diana Rigg and Daniel Craig. If you have arrived at 7a.m., been costumed and made up and then sat around for a couple of hours drinking lukewarm coffee from polystyrene cups, you are already bored before it starts.

Then I discovered that the reason I had been given two costumes was that I wouldn't only be a town crier, but was also required to double up as an 'ordinary' extra and take part in crowd scenes. In fact my Oscar-winning opportunity as a town crier wouldn't take place until the afternoon of the third day. For the first two and a half days I walked up and down the street in crowd scenes. It was all very tedious, but in the process I did learn an important lesson. If you are the person who messes up a scene and makes it necessary for it to be redone, everybody is going to be unhappy with you. This is because, for every thirty seconds of filming, it can take up to thirty minutes to re-set the scene, especially if there are horses and carriages involved, as there often were on the set of *Moll Flanders*. So I resolved that when my big opportunity arrived, I must not mess up.

After two and a half days as just a face in a crowd, my big moment finally arrived. I had observed exactly where the cameras were, and I was determined to play shamelessly for my Oscar. This was to be the scene in which Moll Flanders would steal a purse, be detected, chased after, caught and taken to Newgate Gaol. The scene would open with some general London street action, the primary focus of which would be my town crier proclamation.

So this was it! After two and a half days of waiting, this was my opportunity for stardom! It took a long time for the director to get everything in place: the horse and carriage ready to come down the street, the sedan chair about to be carried up the street, and a lady with a flock of geese ready to cross the street. But finally all was ready, the smoke machine was on and the director uttered the famous words, 'Lights! Cameras! Action!'

I went for it! With a stylish flourish, I began to ring my bell. Scarcely had I finished the second ring when the director yelled 'Cut!' I couldn't believe it. All I had done was ring the bell. How could I have done that wrongly? To make matters worse, this particular director wouldn't speak directly to the extras. He always had his assistant at his side, and if he needed to relay any instruction to an extra, he would give the instruction to his assistant who would then deliver it to the extra. But this made it doubly embarrassing for me. Here I am in my first film, about to deliver my first line, something has gone wrong and all the other actors are watching as the director speaks to the assistant and the assistant then approaches me. He explained, 'David, the director says that the sound of your bell is too loud. It is drowning out all the other street sounds. We won't be able to hear the carriage wheels or the geese or anything but your bell. Can you turn it down?'

I said, 'Well no. My bell doesn't have any settings on it. I'm either ringing it or not ringing it.'

He replied, 'Yes, I thought you might say that. But we simply can't have you drowning out all the other street sounds. So we are going to ask the sound technician to tape up the clapper inside your bell. Then we'd like you to mime the action of bell-ringing for the filming. And if you wouldn't mind staying behind during the next coffee break, the sound technician will record the sound of your bell on a separate soundtrack. He can then mix the sound of the bell at the right level in the final edit, if that's all right with you?'

Well frankly it wasn't all right with me. I had never mimed my bell-ringing before, and haven't done since. But it is difficult to argue with the director when you are only an extra in your first film, and especially with a director who won't even talk to you. What is more, you don't feel fully a man with your clapper taped up. But I had to go along with it.

They set up the scene for the second take. Half an hour later we were again ready for action. I mimed the bell-ringing action, but gave it my all as I launched into my first stentorian 'Ohhh . . . Yezzz!'

'Cut!' yelled the director! I couldn't believe it! A second unidentified blunder on my part has evidently committed us all to another re-take. After two attempts I haven't even got past my first word of dialogue. Daniel Craig,

Diana Rigg and Alex Kingston are looking exasperated, as are all the other actors. The director again speaks to his assistant, and the assistant comes over to me. 'David, the director says that you are shouting too loud. You are drowning out the other street sounds. Can you shout a bit quieter?'

Crushed, I answered, 'Well if it was quiet it wouldn't be shouting, would it?'

He said, 'I understand what you are saying, but we can't have you drowning out the sound of the carriage wheels and the other action. So we are going to have to ask you to mime the sound of your proclamation. Then we will get the sound engineer to record your cry on a separate soundtrack so that we can mix it down to the right level.'

I think he must have seen the look of hurt cross my face as all of my Oscar ambitions were vanishing before my eyes. So he then added something that I know was intended to be kind, but actually just twisted the knife in my heart. He said, 'Don't worry about the lip synchronisation, David. You are only in the background so nobody will notice.'

After another frustrating delay while the scene was reset, we did the scene for a third time. This time with a bell that didn't ring and a crier who didn't cry. It went perfectly. Or, as we professional actors say: 'We got it in the can! It was a wrap!'

That was the last scene of the day's shooting. As we were getting changed out of our costumes I learnt from the other actors that, after six months of filming, this was the very last day. So I naturally ask, 'When will it be on television?' naively thinking they might say something like 'next weekend'. Their actual answer was disappointing. 'Well we now go into editing and post production. It's hard to be precise, but probably it will be in about six months.'

Put yourself in my position at this point. Imagine how it would feel to know that your brilliant film debut is safely on celluloid, but not yet released to the viewing public. You must spend another six months as an unknown before becoming an overnight celebrity. In those circumstances, six months is a very long time. The only productive thing I could find to do in that time was to tell everyone I met, 'Hey I've just made a film with Daniel Craig, Diana Rigg and Alex Kingston. You must look out for it!'

After the longest six months of my life, the Saturday of the first episode finally arrived. It was due to be broadcast at eight in the evening, but by two in the afternoon my wife and I had already buttered the crackers and chilled the wine. At five o'clock we ceremonially removed the brand-new blank video cassette from its cellophane wrapping, having first given blank cassettes to our neighbours on either side, as back-up should anything go wrong with our own recording.

The first episode unfolded. All that is seen of me is a few seconds walking down a street in a crowd scene. More than a little disappointing, I admit, but I consoled myself by thinking that my town crier appearance was likely to be

179

so crucial to the plot that it would appear nearer to the climax. It's just as well I did think that, because the next week I didn't feature at all. In fact, if you put all four one-hour episodes together, all my appearances probably totalled less than twenty seconds, and only my mother recognised me.

You will understand, therefore, that when Moll Flanders was repeated six months later, I refused to watch it as a statement of artistic integrity, which you might better recognise as sulking. However, on the Monday following the repeats, I came downstairs in the morning to find an envelope on my doormat postmarked 'Granada Studios'. Inside the envelope was a substantial cheque for a Repeat Appearance Fee.

Gentle reader, as you now approach the end of this fabulous reading experience, I feel that you and I have become firm friends. I sense that you are a kind and warm-hearted person, always ready to lend a helping hand to your fellow traveller. I wonder if I might therefore ask of you a small favour? Would you now gently lay down this book, pick up a pen and paper, and write a brief letter to Granada Studios telling them how much you would love to see Moll Flanders again? I would greatly appreciate it.

97. The 'Oscar-winning' town crier in *Moll Flanders*

18
POSTSCRIPT

We have reached the end of our journey through the roles of the town crier and bellman, past and present. If you have enjoyed the ride as much as I have, you might not have noticed just how much ground we have covered. We started, as you may recall, with a tour of ancient civilisations. We heard the Ancient Greek crier summoning the citizens to participate in the democratic process. We listened to the Roman *praeco* yelling '*Hoc agete!*' at auctions and trials. And we dropped into the Valley of the Kings to see the Ancient Egyptian scribe-crier Butehamun demonstrating his versatility as both a writer and crier of proclamations.

We found the Bible to be a rich source of precedent for proclaimers, including the earliest mention of a lady crier. And we noted that Jesus' first public statement was to proclaim himself to be . . . a proclaimer.

Arriving on English shores we noted that the bellman tradition was well established before the Norman invasion, even if we were begrudgingly obliged to give the Normans credit for '*Oyez!*' We blew the dust off the *Clare Register of Market Cries* and noted how every aspect of daily life – from straying horses to over-spending wives – came within the vocal remit of the town crier. Gravely we noted that even in death you couldn't do without a proclaimer if you wanted anyone to attend your funeral.

We heard the crier calling out wares for sale – wine, whisky and wives – to name but a few. And we learned how the husbands of over-spending wives would sometimes curb this trait by calling on the local crier to have them blacklisted.

You will probably give an involuntary shudder to recall the long, dark and bitterly cold nights we spent walking alongside the night bellman, enforcing the curfew through the unlit streets of seventeenth-century London, with only a dog for company and a lantern to light the way. You will especially recall the night we spotted a candle still burning in the upstairs window of the house of Mr Pepys. And how the cry we gave that night earned us a fleeting mention in the great man's diary.

Even more famously, I know that you were as thrilled as I was to find yourself rubbing shoulders with William Shakespeare in the crowd that gathered at the High Cross, Cheapside, to hear Robert Cecil proclaim the death of Elizabeth, and the accession of James I.

Grimly we heard the bellman of St Sepulchre's honouring the bequest of William Dowe that the condemned unfortunates of Newgate Gaol should have the good news of salvation proclaimed to them on the eve and morn of their executions.

We became familiar with latchets, jabots and stocks in the outfitting department, as we learnt what the well-dressed proclaimer chose for his apparel.

In the formidable company of Beetty Dick and Mary Ann Blaker, we were loudly reminded that the fairer sex has made, and continues to make, a distinctive contribution to this often male-dominated calling.

It was instructive to spend a day on the streets of Victorian Chester with John Jeffery, and touching to see him reunited with his son. But it was also alarming to hear Jeffery described as 'the last of the city bellmen'. And so it might have proved.

Our story could have ended at that point; the guttering candle was almost snuffed out by the wind of new information technologies. At the eleventh hour we saw how tourism fanned the flame back into life.

Thereafter we stayed in and around Chester and focused on the Chester proclaimers of today. This seemed eminently justified as Chester is the only place in Britain to have retained the tradition of regular midday proclamations from a fixed point – the High Cross. And Chester was the first, and thus far only place, to have chosen its current proclaimers on the basis of their photogenic good looks. Allegedly.

Instead of walking the streets at night to keep visitors out, the current Chester criers walk by day and actively welcome visitors to the city. Rather than dodging the contents of chamber pots, they only have to evade the offbeat questions posed by American tourists.

We have flicked through the diary of the current Chester Town Crier and lingered on some highlights: getting to grips with intercostals, proposing to other men's girlfriends, making revolving horseback proclamations and having his clapper taped up on film sets.

I have enjoyed telling the story of the town crier and bellman and feel privileged to be the first to do so in a full-length book. I believe that two things emerge from the telling. Firstly I hope I have demonstrated that a town crier on the streets of modern Britain isn't just a quaint anachronism, but the continuation of a tradition which has the longest of precedents and a history of indispensable functions. The town crier and bellman permeated almost every aspect of life – and death – in pre-industrial Britain. The neglect of historians to document their roles is a curious oversight, to say the least, but one for which I am grateful. Their omission has allowed me to step into the breach.

Secondly I trust that the latter part of this book has demonstrated that the many and varied roles of town crier and bellman – despite being superseded by newspapers, radio and television – have been reinvented for modern times, and now enjoy a well-merited and vigorous revival. Furthermore, although proclaimers were native to all cultures throughout history, Britain has done more than any other nation to revive the tradition. I hope that you have been able join with me in celebrating this tradition.

Like most accounts, this one has been partial and selective. It isn't the full story, and could never be so. I hope to tell more of the story in subsequent books. If you have any information about historic criers or bellmen from your locality, especially if you have old photographs, paintings, or etchings, I would love to hear from you. Likewise I welcome dialogue on any aspect of the book.

Meanwhile why not come and visit the historic and picturesque City of Chester and allow me to welcome you at the midday proclamation?

Thank you for travelling with me on this journey exploring the roles of the town crier and bellman, past and present. I trust it hasn't been too loud for you.

David Mitchell, Town Crier of Chester
www.chestertowncriers.com
david@chestertowncriers.com

99.

FOR CRYING OUT LOUD!

AFTER DINNER PRESENTATION

LIVE

If audience participation, wit, originality, and continuous laughter are your requirements, David Mitchell is just the After Dinner Speaker for you.

His unique, costumed presentation about life as a town crier has entertained over 400 clubs and societies across the UK, Canada and the USA.

'You are the talk of the club! From start to finish you made it a very special, unforgettable occasion.'
Bramall Park Golf Club

'Without doubt you will rank as one of the most interesting speakers we have had.'
Bournemouth Literary Luncheon Club

'I do not think that I have ever seen the ladies laugh so much or so heartily! People are still coming up to me to say how much they enjoyed your tales.
Cardiff Ladies Luncheon Club

'It was certainly very different from anything we had heard, or seen, before. Several people told me that it was the best ever at the Club. An unforgettable afternoon of brilliant entertainment.'
The Manor Gatehouse Club, Wirral

So, if you are looking for a speaker who is entertaining and amusing, who involves the audience, and who is totally unlike anyone you have heard before, then Chester's Town Crier, David Mitchell, is just the person you need.

Email: david@chestertowncriers.com
Web: www.chestertowncriers.com
Tel: +44(0)1244 311736

NOTES AND REFERENCES

1   This pairing, 'published and proclaimed', was historically very common. It can be found, for example, in *The Taming of the Shrew*: 'For private quarrel twixt your duke and him,/Hath *published and proclaimed* it openly' (Act IV, scene ii). Similarly, Richard II wrote to the Sheriff of Kent on the twelfth day of May 1390: '... we command and charge you that . . . you cause to be published and proclaimed this our ordinance in cities, boroughs, market towns, and other public places within your bailiwick... '

2   Hughes, Thomas, *The Stranger's Handbook to Chester and its Environs*. E.J. Morten, 1856

3   For alerting me to this example, I am very grateful to Dr Mark Collier, Senior Lecturer in Egyptology at the School of Archaeology, Classics and Egyptology at the University of Liverpool

4   The photograph on which our illustration is based was kindly supplied by Bob Partridge, Chairman of Manchester Ancient Egypt Society and Editor of *Ancient Egypt* magazine

5   Proverbs 1:20-21, *Holy Bible, New International Version*. New York International Bible Society, 1978

6   Ibid., Daniel 3:4-5

7   Ibid., Ezekiel 3:1

8   Ibid., Luke 4:16-19

9   Ibid., Mark 4:1-2

10   *Hamlet,* Act V, scene ii

11   Quoted by De Lisle, Leander, *After Elizabeth; How James King of Scotland Won the Crown of England in 1603*, Harper Collins, 2004

12   The Journal of Sir Roger Wilbraham, ed. H.S. Scott. Camden Society, 10, 1902

13   Carey, Sir Robert, ed. F.H. Mares. Oxford University Press, 1972

14   Ibid.

15   *Macbeth*, Act I, scene vii

16   Nichols, John, *The Progresses, Processions and Magnificent Festivities of King James the First, London*, 1828, Vol. 1

17   Ibid.

18   *King Henry VI*, Part III: Act II, scene i

19   *Clare Register of Market Cries* in Court Leet Book of the Manor of the Borough of Clare, 1692–1883. Held by Suffolk Record Office

20   Ibid.

21   Ibid.

22   Quoted by Bullock, David R., *The Ringing Tones of an Ancient Calling*. 1993

23   Quoted by Standage, Tom, *The Victorian Internet; The Remarkable Story of the Telegraph and the Nineteenth Century's Online Pioneers*. Wiedenfeld & Nicolson, London, 1998

24   I am indebted to John Whittle, Editor of *Waverton, A History of its People and Places*, 2002, for alerting me to the Will of Dudley Garenciers

25   Hall, James, *A History of the Town and Parish of Nantwich or Wich-Malbank : in the County Palatine of Chester*. 1883

26   *Staffordshire Advertiser*, 26 June 1824

27   Op cit. Hall, James

28   See Bullock, Connie, *The History of Nantwich Market*

29   *The Winter's Tale*, Act III, scene ii

30   *King Henry IV*, Part 1: Act V, scene i

31   *Chester City Assembly Book*, 13th January 1671

32   Ibid.

33   Ibid.

34   Sampson, Henry, *The History of Advertising*. Chatto and Windus, 1875

35   Lewis, Samuel, *A Topographical Dictionary of England*, 1834

36   Chester Crier's *Book of Precedents* in Chester Record Office

37   Quoted by Bullock, David R, *The Ringing Tones of an Ancient Calling*, 1993

38   Chambers, Robert, Chamber's *Book of Days: A Miscellany Of Popular Antiquities In Connection With The Calendar, Including Anecdote, Biography & History, Curiosities Of Literature And Oddities Of Human Life And Character.* Chambers Harrap, 1832

39   Pepys, Samuel, *Samuel Pepys Diary*, 1660

40   Quoted by Hanson, Neil, *The Dreadful Judgement*. Doubleday, 2001

41   *Chester City Assembly Book*, 13th January 1671

42   Lake, Jeremy, *The Great Fire of Nantwich*. Shiva Publishing Limited, 1983

43   In a letter dated 2 July 1613

44   *Much Ado about Nothing*, Act III, scene iii

45   *Morning Herald*, 30 October 1802

46   *The Times*, 1827

47   *Macbeth*, Act II, scene ii

48   *Minutes for Chester City Assembly* of 1503

49   Op. cit. Chambers, Robert, *Chamber's Book of Days*

50   *A Copy of Verses presented by Isaac Raggs, Bellman, to his Masters and Mistresses of Holbourn Division, in the Parish of St. Giles-in-the-Fields, 1683–4, in The Luttrell Collection of Broadsides.* Held by the British Museum

51   Money, Walter, *A Popular History of Newbury*. W.J. Blacket, 1905

52   Hall, James, *The History of the Town and Parish of Nantwich, or Wich-Malbank : in the County Palatine of Chester.* 1883

53   *Macbeth*, Act V, scene v.

54   Ibid., Act I, scene iii

55   Op. cit. Chambers, Robert, *Chamber's Book of Days*

56   Stow, John, *Survey of London* Second Edition, 1618

57   Strype, John, *A Survey of the Cities of London and Westminster*, 1720

58   Thornbury, Walter, *Old and New London, Volume 2*, 1878

59   *Macbeth*, Act II, scene ii

60   Ibid., Act II, scene ii

61   See Nicholl, Charles, *The Lodger, Shakespeare on Silver Street*. Allen Lane, London, 2007

62   Hanson, Neil, *The Dreadful Judgement*. Doubleday, 2001

63   *Hamlet*, Act I, scene iii

64   Op cit. Proverbs 1:20-21, *Holy Bible*

65   Smith, David R., *Characters of Dalkeith*

66   *The Surrey Herald*, 6 November 1914

NOTES AND REFERENCES

67 I am grateful to Chester historian Gordon Emery who has done much of the spadework unearthing the facts about Chester's criers and bellmen in the Chester Record Office. To anyone wishing to explore the colourful detail of Chester's history I recommend Gordon's books *Curious Chester* and *Chester Inside Out*.

See also www.gordonemery.co.uk

68 Morris, Rev. Rupert H., *Chester*. Society for Promoting Christian Knowledge, 1895

69 *Hamlet*, Act V, scene ii

70 Hughes, Thomas, *The Stranger's Handbook to Chester and its Environs*. E.J. Morten, 1856

71 New, Edmund H., *Chester, A Historical and Topographical Account of the City*. Methuen & Co, London, 1903